CLIFFS&
FENCES

HOLINESS AND PERSONAL SEPARATION
IN BIBLICAL PERSPECTIVE

BY PAUL CROW

CLIFFS&FENCES

HOLINESS AND PERSONAL SEPARATION
IN BIBLICAL PERSPECTIVE

Dedication

I would like to dedicate this book, first of all, to my God. It was He who first burned in my heart a desire to understand personal separation and He who led me to verse after verse of Scripture in search of the truth. My greatest desire for this book, and for life in general, is that both will cause Him to say to me, "Well done."

Second, this book is dedicated to my pastor, Dr. Charles Surrett. He was God's instrument to motivate me to start this project and to see it through to completion. He also has modeled for me, in his preaching and teaching ministry, a balanced, sane approach to Scripture and its application to life.

ACKNOWLEDGEMENTS

I would like to thank my pastor Dr. Charles Surrett for reading the manuscript for me and offering suggestions. Thanks also goes to Mrs. Mary Rosenau, my college English teacher, who was so gracious and meticulous in her insistence upon excellence. I am so grateful for both of these, who were willing to help me make my thoughts communicate better to the intended audience.

An additional thanks goes to all the folks at BookSurge for their technical expertise and willingness to answer every question of a publishing neophyte. Thank you all for helping me to make this goal a reality.

Lastly, I would like to thank my wife for her constant encouragement in this project. She tasted the loneliness of evenings without a husband who was busy working on his book. She knew the value of constructive criticism and the power of honest praise. Throughout this project, she was the friend to me that any wife should be to her husband. She believed my work was quality when I was unconvinced. Thank you, Sweetheart. I love you.

TABLE OF CONTENTS

SECTION I: THE DOCTRINAL BASIS

Section II: Some Specific Issues

INTRODUCTION

As a young man who grew up in independent Baptist churches, I went through the same struggles that many go through as they look at the theological landscape around them. There were times in which I would see a rule in place and wonder why it was there. More importantly, I would wonder what Scripture formed the basis for that rule's existence. After all, if we are going to be truly Baptists, then it is imperative that everything be based upon the Bible; otherwise, we should have the integrity to change our name. A Baptist church that does not stand upon the Bible alone is guilty of false advertising. The Bible, so I was told, speaks to every area of life today, despite having been completed nearly 2,000 years ago. Yet, there seemed to be areas of modern life to which the Bible did not speak. It seemed that men had added to the Scriptures and had made their additions the law in their spheres of influence. While that was tolerable, I suppose, what really bothered me was to see those rules, whose Bible basis I had not ever really seen, change. What had been wrong two years ago was now tolerable. This phenomenon bothered me most of all, particularly because I was convinced that the matter of right and wrong is an absolute. If it had been wrong to do something then, it must still be wrong to do it now. I remember being plagued with questions, most of which I never uttered, but all of which haunted me as I went into college.

It was in college that I finally had some great answers to the questions that had badgered me in high school. After the one particular pastoral theology class in which we looked at the Scriptures pertaining to my questions, I was to eat lunch with the girl who later would become my wife. At that date, I barely touched my food. I talked constantly of the wonderful things that I had just heard in class, barely taking time to breathe, much less eat my food. I was so excited by having Bible answers in the area of standards.

As I look back now that some years have separated me from high school, I believe that I see evidence of many others who struggled with the same questions that I did, only without receiving the Bible answers that I received. Many do one of two things: either they drop out on all service to God, including even simple attendance at church, or they give up the idea of separated Christianity. Those that choose the latter often carry cynicism, if not bitterness, toward any church or individual with standards. It usually isn't long before the calumny of *legalist* is hurled in the direction of anyone who chooses to separate from the world.

In looking at the subject of personal separation from the world, it is necessary to explain an important distinction between separation from worldly activities and isolation from unsaved people. Our Lord was known as the friend of sinners during His earthly ministry, yet He was without sin. The focus of this book does not so much concern itself with separation from people as it does separation from activities. With regard to people, the purpose of association is an excellent litmus test. Do I associate with this person so that I can win him or her to Christ, or do I associate with him or her for the purpose of fellowship? Associating with the unsaved for the purpose of evangelism will tend to create the proper balance between being separated from worldly activities so as to preserve a clear testimony and not isolating oneself so as to preserve evangelistic opportunities. All the separation in the world will bring no one to Christ if the child of God has isolated himself from all contact with unsaved people. Conversely, all the evangelistic opportunities in the world do no good without a testimony of being at least somewhat separate from the world.

If it is right to separate from the world, then there will be Bible evidence for such separation. If there is not Bible evidence for separation, then all who insist on personal separation are no better than the Pharisees and are, in every sense of the word, legalists. This book, then, deals with the matter of what is often called "personal separation": whether or not to wear this garment, whether or not to engage in this activity, whether or not to listen to this, whether or not to watch that. In the first section, this book will attempt to look at the broader issue: Is it right or wrong to live my life according to "standards"? The second section of this book will deal with some specific issues that are often "hot buttons" today. It is my sincere hope that within the pages of this book the reader will see the Bible basis for a life of personal separation from the world.

SECTION I:
THE DOCTRINAL BASIS

Chapter 1:
New Testament Holiness

But as he which hath called you is holy,
so be ye holy in all manner of conversation.
1 Peter 1:15

There was a day when Christianity was known for its distinctiveness in the everyday practices of life. Certain habits of the world were automatically ranked among a list of things that Christians did not do. Almost any unsaved man could have told you that a Christian didn't play card games, go to the movies, dance, drink alcohol, smoke, chew tobacco, use profanity, and a host of other activities common to unsaved humanity. Christian music was decidedly different from the world's music, just as their dress was distinct from the world's dress. There was even a time when some preachers refused to wear wire-rimmed glasses just so that they would not be associated with certain ungodly aspects of the world. There was a day when Christians frowned upon wearing beards, at least in Western culture, because of perceived identification with an ungodly subculture rapidly gaining popularity and becoming ever more vocal in its opposition to core Bible truths. Though some of these rules for living may seem a bit extreme to modern believers, there can be no denying that this form of Christianity was at least outwardly distinct.[1]

Times have changed, however. In Western society today, and particularly in the United States, there has arisen a Christian subculture that is not as distinct as it once was. The days of preaching against movies are all but gone, those applications of Bible separation being now labeled as extreme. No one has a problem with a beard anymore either, provided the one wearing the beard is a man. Card games aren't nearly as wicked as they once were, and smoking is sometimes permitted, as long as it is done outside where no one else has to breathe the smoke. Even alcohol is permitted today, as long as the Christian doesn't get drunk, although no preacher has ever really defined the Biblically acceptable amount of blood alcohol saturation. Music? Well, Christian music is available today that is so much like the world's that its sound is indistinguishable. The unsaved mainstream has long recognized Christian groups who copy popular secular groups in every aspect, from personal appearance to musical style. Only the words they sing are different, for those songs in which the words are distinguishable. Christians love their movies so much that there is now a production house that has dedicated an entire branch of their company to films specifically for the Christian subculture. The movie theater, once a known taboo for any Christian, now receives a great deal of its profits from local professing Christians. If the Christianity of the middle of the twentieth century was distinct from the world, Christianity of the twenty-first century has adopted the chameleon approach: change to blend in with the surroundings. Astute observers in the world know that imitation is the highest form of flattery, and some have even written articles of mockery on the Christian imitations of the day.

Which way is right, according the Scriptures? Perhaps it was extreme to preach against miniskirts, music, and movies. After all, preachers needed to just let people live a little bit and exercise their liberty in Christ, didn't they? If a person gets saved today, it is far better to introduce him to Christian culture that is just the same as the world's culture, only a little bit less vile, right? If becoming a Christian represented a huge change, then no one would ever trust Christ and join the church. After all, the Amish don't make many converts. Is it that important for a Christian to be outwardly distinct from the world? Is it a good thing that you have to talk to a person for a while before finding out that he really is a believer, or should he simply stand out because of what he wears, says, and does? The answer to these questions is found in a very important Bible concept: holiness.

In the early days of Israel's history as a nation, God gave Moses tremendously detailed information about the different aspects of Jewish worship. There were objects to be made, garments to be sewn, and men to be dedicated, all for special duties in the worship of God. When God designated something as belonging to Tabernacle worship, it was to be distinct from everything else in the nation. The term He used to describe any thing or person thus distinguished was *holy*. Once something was purified and made holy, it was dedicated to God forever. In Korah's rebellion, the censers that the rebels used were taken and made into plates for the existing altar. The reasoning was that since the censers had been dedicated to the LORD, they should never be made into anything else that was not totally dedicated to God's service.[2] This passage has been cited as foundational to the Old Testament concept of holiness.[3] The concept first occurs in the Book of Exodus and continues as a recurring theme throughout the Old Testament.

The Levitical worship of the Tabernacle called for certain objects and men to be purified with blood, after which they would be considered holy.[4] After the altar was purified, anything that touched the altar would be also considered holy.

> Transmission of the state of holiness to anything that touched a person or object so consecrated (Exo 29:37; Exo 30:29; Lev 6:18 [H 11], 27 [H 20]) does not necessarily imply that a transferable divine energy exists in the "holy." Rather, it seems that the person or object entered the state of holiness in the sense of becoming subject to cultic restrictions, as were other holy persons or objects, in order to avoid diffusion of the sacred and the profane.[5]

In other words, God put restrictions upon holy things so that everyone would know that there was a difference between something that was common and something that was sacred. In the sense of being distinct from others, Israel was called a holy nation.[6] Many of the regulations that God gave Israel were intended to show to all the surrounding nations that His people were distinct from everyone else. They were uniquely God's people, separated from the rest of the world to Himself for the purpose of bringing glory to Him.

Violation of the separation that was so much a part of holiness was a serious crime in God's eyes, a crime sometimes bringing capital punishment.[7] The details of regulation, not only of the worship proceedings but also of the daily Jewish routine, spoke of God's insistence upon a distinction between the holy and the profane. While there is much in the Old

Testament law that is somewhat unusual to modern readers of the Scripture, it is difficult to miss the fact that the distinction between God's people and the surrounding peoples was very important to God.

The last book of the Old Testament is the prophecy of a man named Malachi. He, like all the Old Testament prophets, spoke for God to the people, usually the people of Israel. By the time Malachi entered the prophetic ministry, the kingdom of Israel had been separated into two kingdoms, Northern and Southern. The Northern kingdom consisted of ten tribes of the original twelve and retained the name Israel. The Southern kingdom consisted of the tribes of Judah and Benjamin and came to be known by the name Judah, the larger of the two comprising tribes. In 722 BC, Israel was taken captive and subsequently repatriated, so that the ten northern tribes effectively ceased to exist as separate recognizable groups. The southern two tribes lasted until 586 BC when they were taken captive as well. After seventy years of captivity, a group from the southern two tribes returned to the land to rebuild first the Temple and then the walls of the city of Jerusalem. Malachi's ministry was to the group of people who had returned to Jerusalem and were living in the land after the Temple and walls had been rebuilt. It was from the pen of Malachi that God gave the most stinging accusation that He ever leveled against His people.

The Book of Malachi is largely in dialogue. God makes an accusation and then predicts the people's response to that accusation. God, through Malachi, then proceeds to prove and/or explain His accusation. Not every accusation evokes a denial from the people of Judah, but many of them do, causing the book to take on a very conversational style between God and His people.

In the middle of this conversational book, God gives a grievous accusation of Judah. He says, "Judah hath dealt treacherously, and an abomination is committed in Judah and in Jerusalem; for Judah hath profaned the holiness of the LORD which he loved, and hath married the daughter of a strange god."[8] This is a serious indictment of God's people, not only because Judah had been raised up to portray God's holiness to the surrounding nations, but most of all because God's holiness was dear to His own heart.

There were outward aspects of Jewish life, as commanded by God, that were designed to reveal to the surrounding nations the fact that God's people were a holy people. The intended assumption was that if Israel (by Malachi's day, they were called Judah) were God's people and their camp and customs were holy, then their God must be holy as well. The more the outward distinctions between the lifestyle of the Jews and the lifestyle of the surrounding people became blurred, the more obscured God's holiness became.

God's holiness has never been a question in heaven. In fact, at this very moment, there are angelic beings circling the throne of God extolling one attribute above all the rest of the many attributes of God: His holiness.[9] When it comes to revealing His holiness on earth, however, God has chosen man to be an important vehicle of revelation. That is, those who know God are to reveal by their difference of life the fact that they are separated from the world and separated to God. In the same way that a mirror reveals a face, God's people are to reveal God's holiness by reflecting it in a holy lifestyle. While mankind can see God's holiness through other means, such as His Word and His judgment on sin, the primary way that ungodly man sees a holy God is by observing the reflection of a holy life. There is a risk in God's plan. If His chosen people abandon their outward distinctiveness, then He has lost the primary way of communicating His holiness to the rest of the world.

God's holiness is dear to His heart, possibly because it separates Him from all the false gods of man's making. When man invents a god, that god is usually just like man, only with a little more power and supernatural ability. The gods of Olympus had their foibles and personal intrigues, just like petty men and women today. The only difference was that they had powers that mere mortals do not possess. It was these powers that elevated them to the status of deity, not their fundamental difference from the men and women who worshiped them. It is not so with the true God of heaven. He is totally separate from any and all sin. He is not a mere man with a little more power. He has never been tainted by sin, nor will He ever be. This attribute of holiness is the only attribute that we are told He loves. To fail to portray the holiness of God is to strike at the heart of God Himself and is evidence of idolatry. By inventing some god who is not holy and does not require holy living, man is violating the second of the Ten Commandments. The deity that a man serves will affect the way he lives his life. Any god that does not require a holy lifestyle is a false god, and any man who worships a god who does not demand holiness is an idolater. By profaning the holiness of the Lord, Judah was evidencing her idolatry. She had traded the God of heaven for another god whose requirements were less stringent and demanding on her daily life.

The Old Testament reveals the progressive violation of God's standard for national holiness as it traces the decline of the Jewish nation. Before Jerusalem was taken captive, one prophet foretold, "I am sought of them that asked not for me; I am found of them that sought me not: I said, Behold me, behold me, unto a nation that was not called by my name."[10] God was saying through Isaiah that there would come a day when God would expand His dealings to people who had not traditionally been associated with the God of heaven. This prophecy was fulfilled in the Church. Today, since the crucifixion and resurrection of Christ, "God commandeth all men everywhere to repent."[11] God's salvation is no longer for the Jews alone, but has been extended to all people in every place. Those who accept this invitation to believe on Christ do not become part of Israel, as converts in the Old Testament did. Instead they become part of what God calls "the church which is His body."[12]

Many of the regulations that were quite essential for Israel to maintain their holy status among the nations are no longer binding on the Church today. In fact, the Holy Spirit Himself in His dealings with church people directly contradicted some of the Old Testament dietary laws that helped set Israel apart.[13] While the Jews are God's earthly people to whom He gave the Scriptures and through whom He gave the Savior, the Church is God's heavenly people. Despite this fact, there are still similarities between Israel in the Old Testament and the Church in the New. One of the most profound similarities is the fact that the Church has temporarily replaced Israel as God's chosen people to portray His holiness to those in this world who do not know Him.

One of the motivations in writing this book is that many in organizations calling themselves churches have "profaned the holiness of the Lord which He loved." Those called of God to display His holiness to the unsaved world have allowed the distinction of conduct to disappear to the place where the world no longer sees the difference. New Testament holiness is more than an outward set of rules and regulations, but like the Jews of old, the believer must demonstrate holiness through the outward difference in his life. Without the outward distinction between Christians and the world, God's holiness is completely hidden to the unsaved.

The New Testament word translated "holy" means "pertaining to being dedicated or consecrated to the service of God."[14] The word was "originally a cultic concept, of the quality possessed by things and persons that could approach a divinity."[15] In other words, just as there were things in Jewish culture that had been set apart for the service of the true God, so Greek culture had persons and objects that were uniquely set apart to approach the pagan deities. To describe this state of being set apart, the Greeks used the word *holy*.

The root concept of holiness in the Scripture includes two ideas that might be described as two sides of the same coin. On the one side, there is negative separation from all that is profane; while on the other side, there is positive separation unto God. Anything that is not separated from sin cannot be separated to God because the essential aspect of God's holiness is that He is separate from sin. The prophet Habakkuk realized this in his prayer to God concerning the coming Babylonian judgment. After realizing the awfulness and adroitness of their military tactics, Habakkuk prayed:

> Art thou not from everlasting, O LORD my God, mine Holy One? We shall not die. O LORD, thou hast ordained them [the Babylonians] for judgment; and, O mighty God, thou hast established them for correction. Thou art of purer eyes than to behold evil, and canst not look on iniquity.[16]

Since the holiness of God precludes the presence of sin, anything that is separated to God must be free from sin.

For the Christian, there is a positional holiness that was a part of God's eternal plan for man's salvation. The Apostle Paul said it this way: "According as he [God] hath chosen us in him [Jesus Christ] before the foundation of the world, that we should be holy and without blame before him in love."[17] God's plan before ever creating man was that all who trust Christ as Savior (thereby being placed "in him") would be made holy and blameless before God, as far as their standing is concerned. This standing is positional holiness. The writer of Hebrews was referring to this positional holiness when he wrote, "Follow peace with all men, and holiness, without which no man shall see the Lord."[18] No man who lacks positional holiness is saved, and no man is saved without also possessing positional holiness. The fact that a man is declared holy at salvation is not a license to live loosely, however. Later on in his Epistle to the Ephesians, the Apostle Paul exhorted, "I therefore, the prisoner of the Lord, beseech you that ye walk worthy of the vocation wherewith ye are called."[19] In other words, since the believer has been made holy before God, his actions should reveal to the world that he is a changed man. The last half of the Book of Ephesians deals with the practical outward manifestation of the inward change that took place at salvation. By the time the reader gets to the fifth chapter of the Book of Ephesians, the idea of personal separation cannot be denied. Paul enjoins, "But fornication, and all uncleanness, or covetousness, let it not be once named among you, as becometh saints; Neither filthiness, nor foolish talking, nor jesting, which are not convenient: but rather giving of thanks."[20] After using the difference between the saved man and the unsaved man as a reason for personal separation, Paul added, "And have no fellowship with the unfruitful works of darkness, but rather reprove them."[21] Clearly New Testament holiness, as presented in the Book of Ephesians, necessitates personal separation. That is, because a man is saved and given blessings in the heavenly places with Christ, there will be some practices on earth that he refuses. The context of the entire Book of Ephesians makes this clear.

In his Epistle to the Romans, Paul again ties the idea of holiness to personal separation. After his classic treatise on the Gospel and its ramifications in the first eight chapters and his discussion of the nation of Israel in the next three, Paul begins to discuss some very practical aspects of Christian living. He implores the Romans, "I beseech you therefore, brethren, by the mercies of God, that ye present your bodies a living sacrifice, holy, acceptable unto God, which is your reasonable service."[22] It is difficult to miss in this wording the similarity to the Old Testament sacrificial regulations. Just as the Jewish sacrifice was to conform to certain standards so as to be holy, so the believer's body must be presented to God in such a manner as to be holy. As in the Old Testament only certain sacrifices were acceptable to God, so there are certain requirements in the believer's life to make him acceptable to God. The next verse elaborates, "And be not conformed to this world: but be ye transformed by the renewing of your mind, that ye may prove what is that good, and acceptable, and perfect, will of God."[23] Clearly, holiness and being acceptable to God are associated with being separate from certain worldly aspects of human existence. As in Ephesians, so in Romans, holiness and personal separation are closely related concepts.

The Apostle Paul was not the only one to link the concepts of holiness with personal separation. Peter, too, under the inspiration of the Holy Spirit, commanded,

As obedient children, not fashioning yourselves according to the former lusts in your ignorance: But as he which hath called you is holy, so be ye holy in all manner of conversation; Because it is written, Be ye holy; for I am holy.[24]

So similar is Peter's command to Paul's in Romans that both men even used the same word to describe the practice of believers patterning themselves after the world.[25]

In all three passages, there are similarities regarding the child of God, holiness, and personal separation. When taken together, these elements instruct the believer in the foundation of personal separation: Biblical holiness.

The first common denominator in the three Bible passages is the contrast between the unsaved way of life and the saved way of life. When Paul told the Ephesians to walk worthy of the vocation wherewith they were called, he was positively asserting that there is a way of life that corresponds with our position in Christ. Since we were placed in Christ at salvation, our conduct should match our position. Later in the chapter, Paul describes the believer's life negatively: "This I say therefore, and testify in the Lord, that ye henceforth walk not as other Gentiles walk, in the vanity of their mind."[26] Clearly, there is to be a difference between the lifestyles of a saved person and an unsaved person.

Paul told the Romans the same thing. He said, "Be not conformed to this world: but be ye transformed by the renewing of your mind, that ye may prove what is that good, and acceptable, and perfect, will of God."[27] The implication is that the world has a plan for living that is different from the will of God for the believer. While the world's plan is to be refused, the will of God is to be adopted.

Peter, too, highlights this contrast of lifestyle: "As obedient children, not fashioning yourselves according to the former lusts in your ignorance: But as he which hath called you is holy, so be ye holy in all manner of conversation."[28] Again, there is the contrast between the way the unbeliever lives, "the former lusts of your ignorance," and the way a believer is supposed to live after salvation, "holy in all manner of conversation." (The word *conversation* here means "way of life, conduct, behavior," and encompasses more than mere words, but deeds as well.[29])

In addition to the contrast between saved and unsaved lifestyles, both authors also apply the word *holy* to the saved person. The Old Testament revealed the consistent difference to be maintained between the holy and the profane, but it also revealed something else about anything that was holy: once God set something apart for Himself, it was to never be used for profane uses again. Even the censers of the rebels were to be recycled back into the use of God's service because they had been sanctified and set apart for Him. The application to the believer is this: once God saves a man, that man no longer belongs to himself. God alone has the right to run his life and direct his daily habits of life, because in salvation, that man was set apart from the world unto God. There will be consequences for every genuine child of God who insists on living a life dedicated to self.[30] Anything once made holy can never be made profane again.

The final similarity is the process given by which the believer's conduct is changed from unholy to holy. In Ephesians, Paul said it this way: "And be renewed in the spirit of your mind."[31] To the Romans, Paul said, "Be ye transformed by the renewing of your mind."[32] Peter worded the same concept slightly differently, "Gird up the loins of your mind."[33] No man will change his actions until he first changes his thinking. The ungodly thought will motivate the unholy action. Therefore, the believer must constantly and consciously change his thinking to conform to the ideas laid out in the Word of God. Once his thinking changes, the actions so characteristic of the unsaved man will fall off of themselves and will be replaced by a life of holiness.

In 1995, I met for the first time the girl who was to later become my wife. Before classes started at the college that we both attended, there was a "Get Acquainted Day" at the local city park. Some students disappeared to the softball diamond, others to the sand volleyball courts, and others to various spots in the shade to remain spectators. I found my way to the sand volleyball courts and had a wondrous time diving for loose balls, filling my pants and T-shirt with sand in the process. During the course of the many games that we played that day, there was a girl who found her way next to me in every rotation. I was talking animatedly throughout the entire course of the games, cracking jokes, and doing all I could to make everyone laugh. To me, this girl was just another person in the crowd that day, at least at first. There came a time, however, when I noticed that she was an attractive girl and that she seemed greatly appreciative of my sense of humor. It was then that my thinking changed. Before noticing this girl, I didn't care if she thought I was funny or not. I said what I said for the benefit of all. After noticing her, however, I found myself checking askance to see if she had been impressed with my latest lame attempt at humor. If she were laughing, I was pleased. By the end of the time, I couldn't care less who else was laughing at my feeble comedic attempts. My thinking had changed to the place where I now did what I did for her benefit alone. As the years went by, I got to know her better and better until the time came when I asked her dad if I could marry her. It was nearly five years after we first met that we did get married. This girl had gone from being just another face in the crowd to the companion of my life, simply because of a gradual change in my thinking.

It should be so with our relationship to God as well. When we first get saved, we know very little of His character, but the more we know, the more our thinking changes. He who was once merely Savior becomes Master and then Friend. Every part of life becomes consumed with pleasing Him. Our thinking has changed from merely seeing Him as a means of escape from hell fire to His being the greatest relationship we will ever have. The more our minds turn toward Him, the greater our desire grows to be like Him in that all-important attribute of holiness.

CHAPTER 2:
THE BATTLEMENT PRINCIPLE

When thou buildest a new house, then thou shalt make
a battlement for thy roof, that thou bring not blood
upon thine house, if any man fall from thence.
Deuteronomy 22:8

In a book dealing with New Testament Christianity, it might be considered a stretch to read a seemingly obscure passage of Old Testament law and presume to find some "hidden" application in it to Church Age saints. As a Baptist, I certainly believe in the hermeneutical principle of distinguishing Israel and the Church. I am fully aware of the error of countless Bible interpreters through the years who have failed to preserve this distinction. At the same time, there are very applicable principles for Church Age saints in the seemingly mundane regulations of the Old Testament law. These laws reveal the character of God and His thinking on matters, so that by analyzing these simple regulations, we can gain spiritual truth.

In his First Epistle to the Corinthians, the Apostle Paul had to deal with a great list of problems that were then confronting the church and hurting its testimony in the community. One of the issues that he addressed was the abuse of a believer's personal rights. In 1 Corinthians 8, Paul had admonished believers to restrict their rights so as to not offend another weaker brother. In 1 Corinthians 9, Paul was going to give a personal example of how he had done in Corinth exactly what he was urging the Corinthians to do to each other: that is, limit his rights so that others would not be offended. In Paul's personal example, it was necessary that he establish the fact that he had a legitimate right to take physical remuneration for his spiritual services. (He had chosen not to use this right so that people could not say that he was motivated materially.) His multi-faceted proof of this right included a reference to a seemingly obscure Old Testament regulation: "Thou shalt not muzzle the mouth of the ox that treadeth out the corn."[34] The Apostle to the Gentiles follows this quotation from Jewish law with some interesting commentary:

> Doth God take care for oxen? Or saith he it altogether for our sakes? For our sakes, no doubt, this is written: that he that ploweth should plow in hope; and that he that thresheth in hope should be partaker of his hope.[35]

For those interpreters of Scripture who insist that both Old and New Testaments should be understood in their normal, literal sense, this passage can present a bit of a difficulty at first glance. It need not present a problem, however.

The regulation was a literal law for literal people using literal oxen to tread literal grain. In the land of Canaan into which the recipients of Deuteronomy were about to enter, grain was essential to the sustenance of each family. In order for the grain to be usable, however, it had to be threshed in order to separate the usable grain from the worthless chaff.

> In some localities several animals, commonly oxen or donkeys, are tied abreast and driven round and round the [threshing] floor. In other places two oxen are yoked together to a drag, the bottom of which is studded with pieces of basaltic stone. This drag, on which the driver, and perhaps his family, sits or stands, is driven in a circular path over the grain. In still other districts an instrument resembling a wheel harrow is used, the antiquity of which is confirmed by the Egyptian records. The supply of unthreshed grain is kept in the center of the floor. Some of this is pulled down from time to time into the path of the animals.[36]

Frugal Jews might be tempted to put a muzzle on the ox so that they could keep all of the wheat for the purpose of human consumption.

Indeed, if this verse did not exist, any man who used a muzzle on his oxen in such circumstances would likely be praised for his foresight. God had a different opinion, however.

By telling Israel that the ox laboring to tread out the corn should be allowed to eat a mouthful every now and then, God was revealing to His people an aspect of His character. Labor and reward are alike important to God. In order to tell His people this aspect of His character, He gave them a mundane law about mundane occurrences of life, occurrences that could illustrate His character when properly understood. The Apostle Paul was trying to convey this truth to the Corinthians in the context of his broader argument, that of limiting his own rights. He says very plainly that God gave this law about grain, oxen, and muzzles "for our sakes, no doubt." God said it for our sakes so that we could understand more about who He is from the laws that He established for His people.

It is important to note that divine law, in the case of oxen and grain, directly contradicted human reasoning. That is, most reasoning men would not want the ox to eat their main source of nourishment before it could even be brought to the table. It just makes good sense to muzzle the ox when he treads out the corn.[37] Many of the laws regarding everyday Jewish life went against human reasoning, illustrating the truth that God would later state through His prophet Isaiah: "My thoughts are not your thoughts, neither are your ways my ways, saith the LORD."[38] In interpreting the significance of Old Testament laws to New Testament believers, it is important to remember two considerations: first, that these laws were literal laws for the everyday life of Israel; and second, that these laws present principles by which New Testament Christians can live, inasmuch as the laws reveal the mind of God.

In the same section of the Book of Deuteronomy, God gave to His people another interesting law that goes against human reasoning. In reference to their future building projects, God said: "When thou buildest a new house, then thou shalt make a battlement for thy roof, that thou bring not blood upon thine house, if any man fall from thence." There are two cultural assumptions made in this verse that are key to a proper understanding, not only to the Jews of that time, but also to Christians of today. First, every new house would have a flat roof, not a pitched roof as seen on modern houses in the West. Second, the flat roof would not only serve to block the sun and rain, but also serve as a gathering place for social, religious, and recreational activities.[39] With these assumptions in mind, it is possible to gain a clearer understanding of God's building code. Since the roof would be flat and since it would be common for many different people to be on the roof, God said that the builder should build a battlement for his roof. The Hebrew word translated *battlement* here simply means a parapet.[40] The parapet would not be so much for defensive reasons in battle as it would be for protective reasons from falling.[41] God said that this protection was mandatory "that thou bring not blood upon thine house, if any man fall from thence."

Like the regulation regarding the ox treading out the grain, this law from God also goes against what might be considered normal human reasoning. No one would fault a man for saying to his children or guests: "You are welcome to go onto the roof with me, but stay away from the edge. If you don't have enough sense to stay away from the edge, then don't go onto the roof in the first place." Although human reasoning would not fault a man for making such a statement, God's reasoning contradicted human reasoning. God reasoned that it was not enough to merely tell people that there was danger on the roof. It was imperative that the Jews go beyond merely expecting people to know where the edge was; they had to build a wall to keep everyone far enough away from the edge so that no one would fall and bring blood upon the house. It was not enough for the owner of the house to merely warn guests of the danger; he had to build a fence.

The battlement principle, then, shows us more of the mind of God. In God's eyes, it is not enough that mankind know of a potential danger; man must also build a fence to keep him from that danger.

CHAPTER 3:
THE CLIFF

All Scripture is given by inspiration of God, and is
profitable for doctrine, for reproof, for correction, for
instruction in righteousness: That the man of God may be
perfect, throughly furnished unto all good works.
2 Timothy 3:16, 17

The title of this book, as might be guessed, is metaphorical. That is, there will be terms used that mean something different from what they might otherwise mean. The first of these metaphors is the cliff. Without a proper understanding of the cliff, it is fruitless to even define, much less try to implement, the fence. For the purposes of this discussion, the cliff is a Bible principle, either directly stated or modeled in the Scripture. Some examples will serve to flesh out both aspects of the definition.

Principles that are directly stated are, perhaps, the most obvious. It is hard to miss the point of verses such as "Thou shalt not commit adultery."[42] If a man commits adultery, he has fallen off the cliff; he has sinned against God. Just as falling off a physical cliff brings dire consequences, so falling off the spiritual cliff brings consequences as well. There are some cliffs from which, if a man fell, he might not live to tell of his experience. In similar fashion there are some spiritual cliffs from which, if a man falls, he is disqualified from certain positions of ministry. Adultery is one such example. In the words of Solomon, "A wound and dishonor shall he get; and his reproach shall not be wiped away."[43] Clearly, anyone who is married and subsequently satisfies his desire for sexual relationship with anyone other than his spouse is directly violating a Bible principle, a principle clearly stated in the Scripture. To this simple commandment Jesus added some divine commentary during His earthly ministry. He told His hearers:

> Ye have heard that it was said by them of old time, Thou shalt not commit adultery: But I say unto you, That whosoever looketh on a woman to lust after her hath committed adultery with her already in his heart.[44]

Without going into all the ramifications of this profound commentary, it is noteworthy that Jesus expanded the Bible principle as traditionally understood. He asserted that the sin need not be physical to still be sin. That is, adultery is as much a mental sin as it is a physical one. No one commits adultery physically without first doing so in his mind. For modern readers of the Scripture, there are profound ramifications of this principle when practically applied. For instance, if what Jesus said was true, it is possible for a man to be watching a football game on Saturday afternoon and, while watching a provocatively dressed woman on a short commercial, commit adultery without ever leaving his easy chair. If such a mental sin were to occur, the man would have fallen off the cliff and sinned against God by violating a clearly asserted Bible principle.[45]

While the Bible principles that are clearly asserted are easy to find, there are other Bible principles that require a more detailed search. Some Bible principles are modeled, rather than directly asserted. For instance, the Bible gives principles of modesty for both sexes in the Old Testament, not by overt assertion, but by modeling the dress of others.

In the Book of Exodus, one of the items God addressed was the implementation of the new form of worship in the tabernacle. There were all kinds of important patterns to follow, not only in the structure of the tent and its worship procedures, but also in the adorning of the men who were to serve in the tabernacle. God, in describing the garments that the priests were to wear, gives a principle of men's modesty. He told Moses: "Thou shalt make them [the priests] linen breeches to cover their nakedness; from the loins even unto the thighs they shall reach."[46] While the sentence of Scripture does not end where the quotation ended and while the main point of the passage is not necessarily a discussion of modesty, there are some guidelines for men's modesty that are modeled in this passage. God said that in order to cover the priest's nakedness, their garments must reach from the loins to the thighs. It is safe to turn this around and state that if the area of the priest's body from his loins to his thighs were exposed, then God would view that exposure as nakedness. Although the years since Moses have drastically changed the fashions of men's apparel, the truth remains that the area of a man's loins to his thighs must be covered. To have this area exposed would constitute nakedness in the sight of God. Thus a principle of men's modesty is present in the Scripture without being preceded by the telltale "thou shalt not."

In like manner the Old Testament Scripture also models principles regarding women's modesty. Isaiah, in addition to prophesying to the nation of Judah, also pronounced coming judgment on other nations in the surrounding vicinity. One such nation was the nation of Babylon. A plethora of different literary devices pour from the pen of the Prince of Prophets, as Isaiah has been called, to convey the meaning of his prophecies. One such device was a form of personification that addressed a hypothetical woman as a representative of the entire nation. The message was one of humiliation and judgment addressed to a woman accustomed to regal treatment.

> Come down, and sit in the dust, O virgin daughter of Babylon, sit on the ground: there is no throne, O daughter of the Chaldeans: for thou shalt no more be called tender and delicate. Take the millstones, and grind meal: uncover thy locks, make bare the leg, uncover the thigh, pass over the rivers. Thy nakedness shall be uncovered, yea, thy shame shall be seen: I will take vengeance, and I will not meet thee as a man.[47]

Part of the judgment of this princess of Babylon would be that she would have to perform the duties of a menial servant girl, specifically grinding meal. In the process, her normally beautifully adorned hair would be uncovered and her legs, specifically her thighs, would be made bare. When these things happened to her, God describes the result in this fashion: "Thy nakedness shall be uncovered, yea, thy shame shall be seen." As in the previous passage, so here there is a Bible principle about modesty, this time pertaining to the woman. If the area of her thigh is uncovered, then that woman is naked in the sight of God. This is another Bible principle that is modeled, rather than directly asserted in the Scripture.

It is at this point in the broader discussion of personal separation that some important questions demand answers. The first question is foundational: What is to be my ultimate authority? The second must also be answered once the first has been decided: Am I willing to bring every aspect of my life under this authority?

Every child of God must decide for himself whether he is going to let the Bible be his ultimate authority or whether he is going to rely on some other source at one point or another. Too many make the mistake of the Reformers who claimed *sola scriptura*, but persecuted those who decided to forsake unbiblical aspects of Reformed doctrine.[48] For the Reformers, the Bible was the absolute authority in some matters of soteriology (the doctrine of salvation), but Catholic tradition supplemented the Bible's authority in other matters. When men came along who questioned and subsequently rejected the aspects of Reformed doctrine based in Catholic tradition, these men were persecuted and some even killed for their insistence upon a Bible basis for theological practice. In the United States today, though there is not currently a climate of religious persecution, there are many that still hold to the Bible in some areas while forsaking it in others.

Too often, the subjects dealt with in any discussion of personal separation are emotionally charged issues. "After all," some query, "how dare any preacher tell me that this skirt is immodest? My grandma bought it for me, and I think it's cute." Similar objections arise when the subject becomes music or entertainment. It is important to realize, however, that all those who have entered into a relationship with Jesus Christ through salvation should want to please Him in every aspect of life. If the Bible truly reveals the mind of God about my dress and I love the God who gave His Son for me, then all He need do is intimate to me that He does not approve of something, and I should be eager and willing to oblige Him. True Bible Christianity does not wait for some long theological proof as to why the Christian must be separate from the world. True Christianity seeks for Christ-likeness for Christ's sake, because of all He did to emancipate the believer from sin.

Now the Christian must proceed to the second question: If the Bible is to be my sole authority, am I willing to give up anything and everything that the Bible speaks against? Am I willing to align myself with God's mind as revealed through His Word? The discussion of standards is absolutely fruitless to any believer who has not answered these questions in the affirmative. All the definitions, proofs, reasons, and explanations about standards do no one any good who has not first decided to surrender to God and His will as revealed in His Word.

Stated another way, any Christian who wishes to benefit from such a discussion as this one on cliffs and fences must first agree that violating a Bible principle is indeed quite analogous to falling off a cliff. The Christian must decide that any violation of God's will for his life is so grievous and brings such awful consequences that such a violation is to be avoided at all costs. Until the child of God comes to this conclusion about the importance of the Bible and how it should direct his daily life, any discussion of standards is wasted time. In fact, the attempted enforcement of standards upon those who do not yet have such a high opinion of the Scripture and its place in Christian living often only serves to harden and embitter those asked to abide by the standards. The Bible as the revealed mind of God must be the only authority for the child of God, and he must be willing to do whatever is necessary to bring his life into conformity with its timeless truth.

CHAPTER 4:
THE FENCE

Enter not into the path of the wicked, and go not in the
way of evil men. Avoid it, pass not by it,
turn from it, and pass away.
Proverbs 4:14, 15

If the cliff is a Bible principle, then the identity of the fence must now be revealed. The fence, or battlement in the analogy of Deuteronomy, is a standard. A standard is a manmade rule for life that is laid down with the intent of preventing the person abiding by that standard from violating a Bible principle. Perhaps one of the most controversial elements of the above definition is the adjective *manmade*. This part of the definition gives rise to two extremes regarding standards, both of which should be avoided.

The first extreme says that it is wrong to ever invent some rule for life and insist that others must abide by it. This, they say, was the error of the Pharisees in Jesus' day. They had multiplied so many manmade rules that they had left off the more important aspects of the Old Testament law. Jesus spared nothing as He rebuked them over and over again during His earthly ministry. Therefore, say those who object to the idea of standards, any manmade rule for life makes the maker of the rule a Pharisee because he has gone beyond what the Bible actually says.

The second extreme would tend to deny that the rule is manmade, insisting rather that it is Bible truth or at least on the same level as Bible truth. Anyone who disagrees with such a position is, in the mind of those who hold it, not right with God and in need of repentance and confession of sin. Often those who hold to this position regarding standards can tend to be unapproachable and unwilling to answer legitimate questions as to the reason for the standard. Curious followers of such men receive answers such as "Because I am the man of God and that is just the way it is" when they dare to ask why some standard is in place. Both extreme positions regarding Bible standards are in error.

The analogy of cliffs and fences is helpful here. If a man were to travel to the Grand Canyon in northern Arizona, he would see the largest natural hole anywhere in the world. Averaging nearly ten miles across and nearly one mile deep, this canyon draws hundreds of spectators each year from all over the world. Along the south rim of the Grand Canyon, the more popular spot for sightseers, there is a path that meanders around the canyon's rim affording visitors different angles for photographing the vicissitudes of color that the sun produces as it rises and sets over the canyon's strata. In between the path and the edge of the cliff in many places is a chain link fence approximately three feet tall. The purpose of the fence is immediately obvious: to keep pedestrians from falling over the cliff into the canyon below. It is entirely possible in places to cross the fence and go out to the extremity of one promontory or another, gain the euphoria of yet another view, and then safely return to one's position on the other side of the fence. While it is possible to cross the fence and still not fall off the cliff, there are dangers other than just the edge of the cliff that the pedestrian must consider. As the trail winds from one point to another, there begin to emerge on the other side of the fence warning signs. The signs state in no uncertain terms that the edge of the cliff is slippery and unsafe to walk on. In other words, if one crosses the fence, he may very well slip and fall, even though the edge of the cliff seems a long ways away.

The path along the south rim of the Grand Canyon, together with its accompanying cliff and fence, provides a great illustration of daily Christian living. The cliff is a Bible principle for life, the violation of which would bring dire consequences just as falling off the rim into the Grand Canyon would bring dire physical consequences. The fence is a standard for life, a manmade rule that prevents the keepers of that rule from ever getting close enough to the cliff to fall over the edge into sin. While it is theoretically possible in places to cross the fence and still not fall off the cliff, there are places where the edge of the cliff is so deceiving that crossing the fence may indeed prove fatal. So it is with standards in the believer's life. There are times when, in theory, one might violate his standard and still not fall into sin. There are also other times, however, when the deceitfulness of sin is so strong that the fence is absolutely necessary, so that crossing the fence in this particular place could mean an almost certain fall. While it is impossible to know how slippery the edge is and whether or not one can safely cross the fence and still be safe from falling, one thing is always certain: the one who never crosses the fence will never fall off the cliff.

Having understood the definition of and reasons for Bible standards, at least one question remains to be answered: Other than the previously cited injunction from Old Testament law, is there any other Bible support for making manmade rules and then living by them? For those who assert that the idea of making and then living by manmade rules is Pharisaical, it might be helpful to examine the first Pharisee.

CHAPTER 5:
THE FIRST PHARISEE?

And the LORD was with Joseph, and he was a prosperous
man; and he was in the house of his master the Egyptian.
And his master saw that the LORD was with him, and that
the LORD made all that he did to prosper in his hand.
Genesis 39:2, 3

The man Joseph is one of the most fascinating characters of all the
Old Testament. Unlike so many other heroes of the Bible, Joseph
is one hero of whom no sins are recorded. It is certain from other statements of Scripture that Joseph was a sinner, for "all have sinned and come
short of the glory of God."[49] Of specific sins, however, Joseph is never once
indicted in the Biblical narrative. A proper understanding of Joseph's story
and response to certain temptations reveals much about the subject matter
at hand.

Joseph was born into a family that could be understated as being
dysfunctional. His father had at least thirteen children by four different
women, two of them slaves and two of them jealous sisters. Jacob, Joseph's father, had a favorite wife, who, when she gave birth, brought forth a
favorite son. The favored wife was Rachel and the favored son none other
than Joseph himself. His brothers' jealousy caused a great many problems
in Joseph's life, but in the end, these problems led to the physical salvation
of the whole family.

Because of Joseph's brothers' jealousy and hatred of him, they sold him
into the custody of Ishmaelite slave traders, who in turn sold him in Egypt
to a military captain named Potiphar, in whose house Joseph served as a

slave. It was as a slave in the military man's house that Joseph met with great prosperity, prosperity that was to become a pattern all during his days of Egyptian servitude.

> And the LORD was with Joseph, and he was a prosperous man; and he was in the house of his master the Egyptian. And his master saw that the LORD was with him, and that the LORD made all that he did to prosper in his hand. And Joseph found grace in his sight, and he served him: and he made him overseer over his house, and all that he had he put into his hand. And it came to pass from the time that he had made him overseer in his house, and over all that he had, that the LORD blessed the Egyptian's house for Joseph's sake; and the blessing of the LORD was upon all that he had in the house, and in the field. And he left all that he had in Joseph's hand; and he knew not aught he had, save the bread which he did eat.[50]

Joseph was not only prosperous and trusted, but he also had another personal trait that was noticed before too much time had expired: "And Joseph was a goodly person, and well-favored."[51]

The former traits made Joseph very attractive to men interested in expanding their estates and personal wealth. With Joseph as manager and the accompanying blessing of the God of heaven upon all that Joseph did, Potiphar was wealthier than ever before. Were Potiphar alive today, he would have been the subject of interviews for the likes of *Fortune 500* or other great financial think tanks.

The latter traits made Joseph attractive to women. Before long, no less of a woman than Potiphar's wife "cast her eyes upon Joseph; and she said, Lie with me."[52] The words are important to note in this particular solicitation. The meaning was that Potiphar's wife wanted to commit adultery with Joseph.[53] It is probably safe to assume that the moral climate of Egypt fell far short of God's standard for morality, as originally given to mankind. Although the written Scriptures had not as yet been given to man, there was God's divine law written on the hearts of men. Even today, one does not need a Bible to be able to tell that adultery is wrong. Even human beings who occasionally eat each other know better than to mess with another man's wife. There can be no doubt that both Joseph and Potiphar's wife knew that adultery was wrong, not only before Joseph's God, but also in the eyes of the Egyptians. In fact, in Joseph's refusal of this woman's proposition, he first appealed to earthly relationships:

> But he refused, and said unto his master's wife, Behold, my master wotteth not what is with me in the house, and he hath committed all that he hath to my hand; There is none greater in this house than I; neither hath he kept back any thing from me but thee, because thou art his wife:[54]

In the end, however, it was Joseph's relationship with his God that seemed to be the greatest deterrent to adultery: "How then can I do this great wickedness, and sin against God?"[55] There can be no doubt that Joseph's answer was a great answer, not only for his time and in his situation, but also for any child of God faced with a temptation to sin. His answer can be summarized as follows: If I sin, it will hurt my standing with men and my relationship to God; therefore, my answer is no.

Some have gotten the idea that Joseph gave this great refusal speech at the initial temptation and then immediately moved on to other things in his life, never to be bothered by this wicked woman again until she finally grabbed his clothing and falsely accused him. If temptation were indeed only a one-time occurrence, there would be no need for standards and certainly not this book. The truth in Joseph's life, as in the lives of all believers, was that temptation kept coming back again and again.

Though the dramatic answer Joseph initially gave can eclipse the next verses, their truth is of great importance to the subject matter at hand: "And it came to pass, as she spake to Joseph day by day, that he hearkened not unto her, to lie by her, or to be with her."[56] Joseph's answer did not drive Potiphar's wife away; it simply made Joseph a greater challenge for this would-be adulteress. Just as temptation comes to believers today, so this woman came to Joseph day by day offering her sin to him. In the face of this onslaught, Joseph realized that simply knowing where the proverbial line was could not, by itself, keep him away from this temptation. Although nothing is said of it in the Biblical narrative, Potiphar's wife, in all probability, did all that was within her power to make herself as attractive to Joseph as she could. So far from being turned away by his initial refusal, she persisted by changing tactics and attempting a compromise. This strategy is one that is often employed by the enemies of God in an effort to wear down the resistance of God's people.[57] The first proposition was to go all the way into immorality: "Lie *with* me." The subsequent proposition was in acquiescence to Joseph's morals: "Lie *by* me." In the first solicitation she was saying "Let's go all the way and be immoral." In the second solicitation her message was entirely different. She was saying the second time: "Joseph, you are tired. Why don't you come and recline next to me and we can unwind at the end of a long day?" She was not asking him to commit immorality this second time. In fact, there is not a verse of Scripture in the entire Bible that comes close to forbidding what Joseph was being asked to do. Nowhere would God ever say, "Thou shalt not recline next to a person of the opposite gender." Yet, when given the opportunity to recline at the end of the day and talk to this woman about seemingly innocent household affairs, Joseph again refused. His refusal did not end the temptation or the offered compromises, however.

Potiphar's wife, like all promiscuous women in Scripture, was persistent. If Joseph's morals prohibited him from adultery and his standards precluded his reclining in her company, then she would try something completely innocent that would arouse the suspicion of no one. Her final compromise was "*Be with* me." What could be more natural than the lady of the house wanting to know more about the affairs of the estate? What possible moral harm could exist in walking around the perimeter of a grain field in the flood plain together or examining the stalls of animals in company? Certainly nothing in culture would preclude such a liaison. In fact, though the Scripture was unavailable to Joseph, God's revealed Word had no prohibitions of this kind of harmless conversation. Surely no one would claim to find a prohibition such as, "Thou shalt not be with someone who is not thy spouse," anywhere in either Old or New Testaments. Yet Joseph refused even this invitation.

Joseph was doing exactly the same thing that Pharisees of Jesus' day practiced: he was living by an extra-Biblical rule for life. While we are all glad that Joseph never did sin with his master's wife, he surely could have lightened up a bit. To think that Joseph is so often upheld as an example of how to behave, and that to young people, is almost disconcerting, considering that Joseph lived by rules that are never stated in Scripture. He, in reality, seems to have been the first Pharisee.

Or was he? Was Joseph adding rules that can never be found in Scripture to his personal life just so that he could flaunt his adherence to a manmade code? While this may seem true on the surface, a second look at the situation reveals deeper meaning and even wisdom in what Joseph did in response to his temptress. Just as the cliffs of the Grand Canyon are sometimes more slippery than they seem, so sin, particularly adultery, is more mesmerizing than its victims at first realize. While Scripture does not ever prohibit being with a person of the opposite gender, it does give commands like these: "Flee fornication"[58] and "Flee also youthful lusts."[59] While there might not have been a sin in taking a walk with this wicked woman, it would be one step toward the slippery edge of the cliff of adultery. In order to protect himself, Joseph built a fence a long way back from the slippery edge of the cliff: he refused to be with this woman at all.

Some teachers and preachers who are critical of anyone who forms standards in his life are full of praise for the man Joseph and his refusal of so many onslaughts of so wicked a woman. Does not honesty to the text dictate that we at least acknowledge Joseph's manmade rules for life? Joseph first of all understood the cliff and the dangers of falling over that cliff. Adultery would not only destroy his standing with man, but it would mar his relationship with God. Because the consequences of falling off the cliff were so serious, Joseph decided to build at least two protective fences, the second more protective than the first. No thinking child of God can deny the effectiveness of Joseph's fences in keeping him from the cliff.

Although centuries of history and cultural change separate modern Christianity from Joseph and the Egyptians, the young Hebrew's example is still as relevant today as it was to Old Testament Jews. Like Joseph, every child of God must build fences. It is not enough just to know that something God prohibits is sin. There are times when, in order to avoid falling into sin, the child of God must create some rules for his life so that he will never have the opportunity to violate those important Bible principles. It is not enough just to know where the edge of the cliff is and to stay away from it; you must also build a fence.

CHAPTER 6:
WHAT IS A PHARISEE?

Then spake Jesus to the multitude, and to his disciples,
Saying, The scribes and the Pharisees sit in Moses' seat: All
therefore whatsoever they bid you observe, that observe and
do; but do not ye after their works: for they say, and do not.
Matthew 23:1–3

It might be misconstrued from the last chapter that this book endeavors to paint the Pharisees of Scripture in a positive light or that Joseph was the first member of that group. In reality, the mention of Joseph as a Pharisee was a tongue-in-cheek reference designed to motivate the reader to weigh what he might have always thought against what the Bible says about Joseph. If Joseph, despite living his life according to extra-Biblical rules, was not a Pharisee, and if he is rightly upheld as a positive rather than negative example of godliness, then what differentiates Joseph from the Pharisees of Jesus' day? To be sure, any casual reading of the Gospel accounts will reveal scathing denunciations of the doctrine and practice of the Pharisees, denunciations originating from no less than the Savior Himself. To put the problem simply, the Pharisees were bad and Joseph was good. Since they did some of the same things, what was it that made them so fundamentally different? In order to answer this question, it will be necessary first to take a look at the group known in the New Testament as the Pharisees.

Though the history of the Pharisees is extensive and sometimes even controversial, it is also beyond the purpose of this particular discussion and will be left largely untouched here. The scope of this book concerns itself only with the Pharisees as they are represented in the Scriptures in general and in the Gospels in particular.

It is necessary to realize that the Pharisees were very doctrinally similar to Christians in many respects. Though this may seem shocking considering the negative picture given of the Pharisees, an examination of the Scripture seems to support the fact that there was at least some doctrinal common ground between the two groups.

The Pharisees, unlike some of the more secular Jews of the First Century, seemed to be looking for the promised Messiah. When Herod inquired of the place of Messiah's birth, there were scribes ready to provide a Bible answer to the king's question:

> And when he had gathered all the chief priests and scribes of the people together, he demanded of them where Christ should be born. And they said unto him, In Bethlehem of Judea: for thus it is written by the prophet, And thou Bethlehem, in the land of Judah, art not the least among the princes of Judah: for out of thee shall come a Governor, that shall rule my people Israel.[60]

These scribes may not have been Pharisees, but Jesus, during His later public ministry, would seldom mention the Pharisees without including the scribes in His rebuke. Clearly, these scribes of Herod's day were keenly aware of the Messianic prophecies of the Old Testament Scripture, and history indicates that the Pharisees likewise were knowledgeable about the coming Messiah. Some assert that the Pharisees did much to keep the Messianic hopes of the Jews in front of the people during the time of Christ.[61] Even the woman at the well, though she doubtless would have been shunned by the Pharisees for many reasons, was at least vaguely familiar with the Messianic hope: "I know that Messias cometh, which is called Christ: when he is come, he will tell us all things."[62] She had somehow been reminded of the truth of the coming Messiah, even in her village of hated Samaria. It could have been that the Pharisees had been influential in this reminder. In their Messianic hopes, then, the Pharisees bore similarity to Christians in doctrine.

The Pharisees also held to a high view of the Scripture. To be sure, they had missed some of the most important concepts of the Law, but they did know the Law, particularly its prohibitions. Paul's discussion of the number of one Hebrew word in the Old Testament has been held up as a classic example of Pharisaical exposition:[63] "Now to Abraham and his seed were the promises made. He saith not, and to seeds, as of many; but as of one, And to thy seed, which is Christ."[64] If the Pharisees held a high regard for Scripture, they held some common ground with Christians. In Berea, those who highly esteemed the Scriptures were termed "noble" by Luke, the first Christian historian.[65] Later on, the Apostle Paul would tell Timothy:

All Scripture is given by inspiration of God, and is profitable for doctrine, for reproof, for correction, for instruction in righteousness: That the man of God may be perfect, throughly furnished unto all good works.[66]

In reality, the Pharisees knew far less about the Scripture than they pretended to know, but they at least doctrinally held to a position of Biblical authority.

The Pharisees also believed in the resurrection and the existence of spirit-beings or angels. The Apostle Paul, in his defense before the Jews in Jerusalem, appealed to his doctrinal beliefs, beliefs that he had held as an unsaved Pharisee and retained as a Christian Apostle.

But when Paul perceived that the one part were Sadducees, and the other Pharisees, he cried out in the council, Men and brethren, I am a Pharisee, the son of a Pharisee: of the hope and resurrection of the dead I am called in question. And when he had so said, there arose a dissension between the Pharisees and the Sadducees: and the multitude was divided. For the Sadducees say that there is no resurrection, neither angel, nor spirit: but the Pharisees confess both.[67]

This defense ended up dividing his accusers and eventually broke up his trial by dissolving it into pandemonium. The belief in both doctrines, however, is vital in Christianity. Indeed, the doctrine of the resurrection, first of Christ and subsequently of all men, may be called the quintessential doctrine of Christianity. Likewise the existence of spirit-beings or angels, asserted often in the Old Testament, is reaffirmed in the New Testament as well. Here again, the Pharisee and the Christian have some common doctrinal ground.

In spite of the doctrinal similarities between the Pharisees and Christians, the majority of the New Testament references to the Pharisees are decidedly negative. The reason for this is that similarity to right doctrine is still error; in order to avoid error, there must be identity with right doctrine. The Pharisees' errors did not stem from their common ground with Christians; they came from their aberrations from and additions to right doctrine.

A sampling of the references to the Pharisees reveals the negative attitude toward them in the Gospel narrative.

But when he [John the Baptist] saw many of the Pharisees and Sadducees come to his baptism, he said unto them, O generation of vipers, who hath warned you to flee from the wrath to come?[68]

For I say unto you, That except your righteousness shall exceed the righteousness of the scribes and Pharisees, ye shall in no case enter into the kingdom of heaven.[69]

But woe unto you scribes and Pharisees, hypocrites! For ye shut up the kingdom of heaven against men: for ye neither go in yourselves, neither suffer ye them that are entering to go in.[70]

Since there was so much doctrinal similarity between Christian and Pharisee, why would New Testament writers take so much pain to distance the Christ of Christianity from Pharisaical dogma?

The primary error in the Pharisees' practice was their great emphasis on the externals without regard to internal reality. While maintaining a strict exterior separation from those who so much as disagreed with their unique interpretations of the Law, they all the time either had no spiritual reality or else were full of vile wickedness before God. This error stemmed from a problem with authority: while they believed the Old Testament Scriptures as an authority, it was not, for them, the only authority.

The Pharisaic theory of tradition was that these additions to the written law and interpretations of it had been given by Moses to the elders and by them had been transmitted orally down through the ages. The classical passage in the Mishna is to be found in Pirqe' Abhoth: "Moses received the (oral) Law from Sinai and delivered it to Joshua and Joshua to the elders, and the elders to the prophets and the prophets to the men of the great synagogue." Additions to these traditions were made by prophets by direct inspiration, or by interpretation of the words of the written Law.[71]

Jesus took the words of Isaiah, so familiar to the Pharisees, and used them to expose Pharisaical error: "This people draweth nigh unto me with their mouth, and honoreth me with their lips; but their heart is far from me. But in vain they do worship me, teaching for doctrines the command-ments of men."[72] Thus, for them, the problem was not that they believed the Law, but that they also held as authoritative the words of men.

As is always the case when man's word becomes authoritative, it was not long before they forgot the words of God and paid more attention to the words of men in their daily lives. The result was a greater and greater emphasis on externals and less of an emphasis on real righteousness before God. As the generations passed, the Pharisees focused less and less on real righteousness as defined in the Scripture and more and more on the false righteousness of the external. The less they focused on real righteousness, the more truly wicked they became within.

The outer show combined with the inner wickedness of their hearts brought forth the repeated charge of hypocrisy from the lips of the Savior. The Jews around them saw that they were obviously in accordance with the Old Testament law, but only God could see the wickedness of their hearts. The Pharisees wanted to make sure that no one missed their exterior godliness, so much so that they would go to great lengths to display it. For example, they would "make broad their phylacteries, and enlarge the bor-ders of their garments."[73]

Before explaining the theological significance of this verse, it would be helpful to define the phylactery and the border of the garment and give their intended application. The practice of the phylactery was based upon four Old Testament verses: Exodus 13:9, 16; Deuteronomy 6:8; 11:18.

The phylactery was a leather box, cube-shaped, closed with an attached flap and bound to the person by a leather band. There were two kinds: (1) one to be bound to the inner side of the left arm, and near the elbow, so that with the bending of the arm it would rest over the heart, the knot fastening it to the arm being in the form of the Hebrew letter *yodh* (y), and the end of the string, or band, finally wound around the middle finger of the hand, "a sign upon thy hand" (Dt 6:8). This box had one compartment containing one or all of the four passages given above. The writer in his youth found one of these in a comparatively remote locality, evidently lost by a Jewish peddler, which contained only the 2nd text (Ex 13:11–16) in unpointed Hebrew. (2) Another was to be bound in the center of the forehead, "between thine eyes" (Dt 6:8), the knot of the band being in the form of the Hebrew letter *daleth* (d), with the Hebrew letter *shin* (sh) upon each end of the box, which was divided into four compartments with one of the four passages in each. These two Hebrew letters, with the yodh (y) of the arm-phylactery (see (1) above), formed the divine name Heb: *shadday*, "Almighty." Quite elaborate ceremonial accompanied the "laying" on of the phylacteries, that of the arm being bound on first, and that of the head next, quotations from Scripture or Talmud being repeated at each stage of the binding. They were to be worn by every male over 13 years old at the time of morning prayer, except on Sabbaths and festal days, such days being in themselves sufficient reminders of "the commandment, the statutes, and the ordinances" of Yahweh (Dt 6:1).[74]

The borders of their garments were likewise a reaction to something in the Old Testament law. God had told Moses:

Speak unto the children of Israel, and bid them that they make them fringes in the borders of their garments, throughout their generations, and that they put upon the fringe of the borders a ribband of blue: And it shall be unto you for a fringe, that ye may look upon it, and remember all the commandments of the LORD, and do them; and that ye seek not after your own heart and your own eyes, after which ye use to go a-whoring:

That ye may remember, and do all my commandments, and be holy unto your God.[75]

This passage, in all likelihood, was to be literally obeyed.

When God said that certain things were to be as frontlets between the eyes and a sign upon the hand, He was speaking figuratively. The Pharisees, in their desire for visible outward conformity, misinterpreted these passages and turned them into another opportunity to flaunt their supposed spirituality. It was not enough for them to wear phylacteries; they had to augment them so as to make them more visible.

Although the fringes on the borders of garments were to be literal, the Pharisees erred in their purpose of this observance. The purpose for the fringe was not open for discussion: "that ye may look upon, and remember all the commandments of the LORD, and do them." In God's eyes, a person could go through his entire life with none but himself seeing his fringes, and the fringes would still serve their intended purpose, so long as the wearer remembered God's commandments. The purpose of the fringe was for none but the wearer himself. Instead, the Pharisees wanted to be seen by men as spiritual and so made the borders and the fringes as large as they possibly could, not for their own eyes, but for the eyes of others. The motive, rather than the action, was the problem.

While those who surrounded the Pharisees saw them as being in perfect accordance with the Law, God saw them for what they were on the inside. On the inside, they wanted no mercy for those who did not meet with their standard. Accordingly, they accosted the disciples when Christ ate with publicans and sinners.[76] While others saw the Pharisees as generous, God saw that actually they were "full of extortion."[77] While others saw the Pharisees as the most likely candidates for heaven, God saw their lost condition.[78] While others saw the great prayers of the Pharisees, God saw their inner covetousness.[79] While others saw their missionary zeal, God saw the damage they did by bringing another to hell.[80]

In short, to call a person a Pharisee is a grievous slander, to this day. The Pharisees, having accepted an authority in addition to the Bible, grew more and more outwardly rigid while becoming more and more inwardly wicked. Any man that advocates the life of a Pharisee is in direct opposition to all that the Scripture, both Old and New Testaments, advocates for mankind.

The logical question demands an answer then: What is the difference between Joseph and a Pharisee? So far, the following have been asserted as facts:

- Joseph is the prime example of a man right with God.
- The Pharisee is an example of someone who was consistently condemned by God.
- Both of these lived by extra-Biblical rules for their lives.
- Believers today must formulate and live by extra-Biblical rules for their lives.

Assuming that all of these are true, the distinction between Joseph and the Pharisee takes on prime importance.

CHAPTER 7:
VIVE LA DIFFERENCE!

For I desired mercy, and not sacrifice; and a knowledge of
God more than burnt offerings.
Hosea 6:6

The difference between Joseph and a Pharisee is one of the heart. The statement of refusal by Joseph gives great insight into his heart's motivation: "How can I do this great wickedness and sin against God?"[81] To be sure, Joseph was concerned with how his sin would affect other people, but the sin was ultimately a sin against God. By contrast, the Pharisees had a different motivation altogether: "All their works they do for to be seen of men."[82] This motivation is the difference between a sterling life of separation from sin in the case of Joseph, and a disgusting life of hypocrisy in the case of the Pharisees.

Early in Christ's ministry, He confronted the Pharisees with a tremendous verse of Scripture that brought their root problem to the surface. The first instance of the quotation came in response to the Pharisees' accosting the disciples:

> And it came to pass, as Jesus sat at meat in the house, behold, many publicans and sinners came and sat down with him and his disciples. And when the Pharisees saw it, they said unto his disciples, Why eateth your Master with publicans and sinners? But when Jesus heard that, he said unto them, They that be whole need not a physician, but they that are sick. But go ye and learn what that meaneth, I will have mercy, and not

sacrifice: for I am not come to call the righteous, but sinners to repentance.[83]

Had the Pharisees really had a relationship with God, they would have known that He loves to show mercy and thus to give men more space to repent. Jesus brought this fact to light by quoting a verse of Scripture that they had read many times but never understood. When Hosea spoke of "sacrifice," he was referring to the outward conformity to the Old Testament law. In the Hebrew parallelism, the phrase "burnt offerings" refers to the same thing. Hosea had spoken for God hundreds of years earlier, but the Pharisees did not know the meaning of what Hosea had penned. The problem was a lack of inward relationship with God.

There was another time when the Lord brought the same verse to bear in dealing with the same group, the Pharisees. The second infraction, in the eyes of the Pharisees, concerned a Sabbath violation.

At that time Jesus went on the Sabbath day through the corn; and his disciples were an hungered, and began to pluck the ears of corn, and to eat. But when the Pharisees saw it, they said unto him, Behold, thy disciples do that which is not lawful to do upon the Sabbath day. But he said unto them, Have ye not read what David did, when he was an hungered, and they that were with him; How he entered into the house of God, and did eat the showbread, which was not lawful for him to eat, neither for them which were with him, but only for the priests? Or have ye not read in the law, how that on the Sabbath days the priests in the temple profane the Sabbath, and are blameless? But I say unto you, That in this place is one greater than the temple. But if ye had known what this meaneth, I will have mercy, and not sacrifice, ye would not have condemned the guiltless. For the Son of man is Lord even of the Sabbath day.[84]

Once again, the Pharisees insisted on outward conformity without giving the first thought to the inner needs of man. Had they understood God's emphasis on the inward man, as opposed to the exterior, they would not have made such an accusation.

There can be no doubt that God's first concern is for the inward part of man, frequently called the heart. In fact, the Old Testament is replete with expressions of God revealing His desire for purity of heart. The same Law that the Pharisees loved to quote emphasized the heart relationship over the outward appearance. As Moses stood at the brink of the Promised Land after the years of wandering in the wilderness, he reminded Israel: "Thou shalt love the LORD thy God will all thine heart, and with all thy soul, and with all thy might."[85] The Law also gave some interesting commands regarding the heart attitude of one man for another: "Thou shalt not hate thy brother in thine heart: thou shalt in any wise rebuke thy neighbor, and not suffer sin upon him."[86] This command about not hating a man in the heart is in a series of prohibitions that tell God's people how they are to treat their fellow man. In the very next verse, God gives the great summary, "Thou shalt love thy neighbor as thyself." All the outward commands given to Israel were tied to something very inward: love for God and man. Love is an inward thing, whereas the majority of the commands given were outward. According to Jesus, the command to love God above all else and love one's neighbor as oneself were the two great commandments on which all the law and prophets were based.[87] The heart was the main concern, more than the outward actions.

As Old Testament revelation progressed, this emphasis on the heart condition of man only increased through the ministry of the poets and prophets. Samuel, after helping Israel to choose a king, urged the people, "Only fear the LORD, and serve him in truth with all your heart: for consider how great things he hath done for you."[88] The balance between the inward and outward is present, with the inward getting special emphasis. Samuel says to serve God (an outward action) in truth (an inward action) with all of your heart (an inward motivation). While there is mention of the outward action, there is also the great emphasis on the heart.

David the King was known as the man after God's own heart.[89] Whereas others urged Israel to have a pure heart, David prayed for it in his many recorded psalms. After considering the revelation of God to man, David prayed, "Let the words of my mouth, and the meditation of my heart, be acceptable in thy sight, O LORD, my strength, and my redeemer."[90] After considering the greatness of God, David asked a question and then answered it: "Who shall ascend into the hill of the LORD? Or who shall stand in his holy place? He that hath clean hands, and a pure heart; who hath not lifted up his soul unto vanity, nor sworn deceitfully."[91] Again, there is mention of both the exterior, clean hands, and the internal element, a pure heart. The verse, however, seems to put especial emphasis on the internal: "Who hath not lifted up his soul unto vanity, nor sworn deceitfully." While the latter part of this quotation can include the outside actions of man, both elements are chiefly concerned with who man is on the inside. When David sinned with Bathsheba and was subsequently confronted by the prophet, he repented of his sin and included in his penitential psalm these words: "Behold, thou desirest truth in the inward parts: and in the hidden part thou shalt make me to know wisdom."[92] Later he requested, "Create in me a clean heart, O God; and renew a right spirit within me."[93] As if this were insufficient to express the emphasis of the matter, he prayed later in the psalm:

> For thou desirest not sacrifice; else would I give it: thou delightest not in burnt offering. The sacrifices of God are a broken spirit: a broken and a contrite heart, O God, thou wilt not despise.[94]

If God is concerned with the heart and David was a man after God's own heart, it is no wonder that the king of Israel would pray such things. David understood that God really didn't care so much about exterior conformity to regulation as He did about internal brokenness over sin.

Solomon, too, though his heart was turned away from serving God,[95] nevertheless wrote these words under inspiration of the Holy Spirit: "The sacrifice of the wicked is abomination: how much more, when he bringeth it with a wicked mind?"[96] The message is still the same: if the outside is right and the inside is not, it disgusts a holy God.

In spite of this desire of God's heart as revealed through David's psalms and Solomon's proverbs, Israel developed a growing pattern of outward conformity without inward substance. The Pharisees, in fact, were simply the next in a long line of Jews who outwardly conformed but inwardly rebelled. Hundreds of years before the birth Christ, God had told Judah through Isaiah:

> To what purpose is the multitude of your sacrifices unto me? saith the LORD: I am full of the burnt offerings of rams, and the fat of fed beasts; and I delight not in the blood of bullocks, or of lambs, or of he goats. When ye come to appear before me, who hath required this at your hand, to tread my courts?

Bring no more vain oblations; incense is an abomination unto me; the new moons and Sabbaths, the calling of assemblies, I cannot away with; it is iniquity, even the solemn meeting. Your new moons and your appointed feasts my soul hateth: they are a trouble unto me; I am weary to bear them. And when ye spread forth your hands, I will hide mine eyes from you: yea, when ye make many prayers, I will not hear: your hands are full of blood.[97]

God was not telling Israel that He was not concerned with outward obedience so much as He was telling them that outward obedience without inward heart was repulsive to Him.

Hosea, one of the minor prophets (so called because his writing ministry was shorter than that of the major prophets), continued this line of truth as he spoke for the God of heaven to the northern tribes of Israel. He lamented, "They have not cried unto me with their heart, when they howled upon their beds,"[98] and later, "Their heart is divided."[99] He was saying that, although Israel cried to God, they were not wholehearted in their cries. Joel, another minor prophet, urged the people:

Therefore also now, saith the LORD, turn ye even to me with all your heart, and with fasting, and with weeping, and with mourning: And rend your heart, and not your garments, and turn unto the LORD your God: for he is gracious and merciful, slow to anger, and of great kindness, and repenteth him of the evil.[100]

The problem in Joel's day was that the people would rend their garments as an outward sign of repentance, but their outward show was insincere. God through Joel told them to rend their heart. In other words, God really couldn't care less whether or not their garments were rent, so long as they were genuinely repentant in their hearts.

It would seem that by the time Jeremiah prophesied to the people, they had thrown off much of the outer semblance of worship for God. Their evil hearts had finally overcome their hypocrisy to the place where there was very little left of outward show. Still Jeremiah pleaded with Judah to give their heart to God: "O Jerusalem, wash thine heart from wickedness, that thou mayest be saved."[101] After prophesying judgment against Judah and Jerusalem, Jeremiah proclaimed, "Thy way and thy doings have procured these things unto thee; this is thy wickedness, because it is bitter, because it reacheth unto thine heart."[102] In other words, the actions that brought the judgment of God came from a wicked heart. They were not slips or accidents, but rather premeditated actions that revealed a wicked heart.

John the Baptist and then Jesus Himself said nothing that the prophets had not attempted to tell the people for centuries. While the Babylonian captivity had removed from Judaism its penchant for polytheism, the old problem of outward conformity from a wicked heart persisted in the days of John and Jesus. Therefore, they went forth with a message of repentance. The change needed to be within, from the heart.

Without a doubt, the heart is most important to God; but that does not mean that exteriors are unimportant. While Jesus constantly rebuked the Pharisees for their outward conformity from a wicked heart, He did commend them on at least one occasion for their meticulous outward observance of the Law: "Ye pay tithe of mint and anise and cummin, and have omitted the weightier matters of the law, judgment, mercy, and faith: these ought ye to have done, and not to leave the other undone."[103] Jesus was not saying that it was wrong to tithe so meticulously. He said that they should have done judgment, mercy, and faith—weightier things that they had omitted—and still have tithed the way they did. This represents a very important balance and sums up the difference between Joseph and the Pharisees. Joseph had an outward righteousness, even to the point of making extra-Biblical rules for himself to keep him from sin against God. The Pharisees also had an outward "righteousness" composed of extra-Biblical rules to which they meticulously adhered. The difference was one of the heart. To Joseph, the very thought of breaking the heart of God by sinning against Him led him to do whatever was necessary to keep from sin. The Pharisees cared nothing for God's opinion, choosing rather the praise of men as the reward for their actions.

The Pharisees' philosophical approach to life did not die with the Jews who bore that name. There are many people who are Christians today who work by the same principle as the Pharisees. They, like the Pharisees, live by manmade standards so that other men can see them and think them spiritual. It was not their standards that were wrong in and of themselves, but the motivation behind these standards. If a man's motivation for building fences is to hear other men sing his praises, then God is just as repulsed by such a man as He was by the Pharisees.

On the other hand, when a man gets close to God and sees the awfulness of sin, he is willing to do whatever is necessary to keep himself from that sin. He looks at life with the philosophy of Joseph: *How can I do this great wickedness and sin against God?* He creates rules for himself that he plans to keep, regardless of whether anyone sees him keeping them or not. They apply not only in the public arena, but also in the private sector of life, because the motivation for those rules is not the approval of fickle men who cannot always see, but the approval of the immutable, omnipresent God.

In writing this book, one of my greatest desires is that the difference between Joseph and the Pharisees be upheld and vigorously maintained. There are more options than just being worldly or being a Pharisee. As in so many other areas of life, the truth is found at neither extreme, but in a balance of the two. The concept of a life of standards on the outside and a heart right with God on the inside is not an either/or proposition; it is a both/and proposition. Both the inside and outside are important to living a life of godliness.

CHAPTER 8:
BORDER DISPUTES

But if thy brother be grieved with thy meat, now walkest
thou not charitably. Destroy not him with thy
meat for whom Christ died.
Romans 14:15

As a boy, growing up in suburban America, I remember the time when my dad decided to install a privacy fence around our backyard. The wood fence itself came in sections eight feet long by six feet tall. Every eight feet, we would put a four-by-four post in the ground to which to attach the sections of fence. During the installation process, Dad took a long string and ran it all the way down the length of our property, attaching the string to two stakes. He drove one stake in at one surveyor's marker and another stake in at the other surveyor's marker on the other side of our property. While we were installing the fence, he told us that we should never let the fence touch the string. We were to get close to the string, but never touch it, lest by touching we begin to move the string and so encroach upon the neighbor's property. After the fence was all in place, we discovered that one of our neighbors did not share our excitement in the project's completion. He evidently told my dad that fence should have been built more on our property than on the property line. Whether Dad told him of our string and the meticulous way that we had avoided going onto his property or not, I cannot remember. What I do remember is the dispute over the fence.

One day, our neighbor's teenage son—or one of his friends—smashed one section of fence with his car. Dad, upon discovering the problem, took some tools and some wood onto the neighbor's property to repair the fence. I do not remember all that the neighbor said that day, but the encounter was not the high point of our neighborly relationship. I do remember that the neighbor told my dad, "Crow, I ought to just get my gun and shoot you." Evidently, this announcement did not have the desired effect, so he inquired, "What are you going to do?" My dad was undaunted. "I'm going to fix my fence." We never saw the gun that day or any other day, for that matter, and that incident represented both the climax and the culmination of our dispute over the fence. Not long after, the neighbor came to Dad and said, "Crow, you're all right," and things were more or less fine until the day he moved out.

In the United States, border disputes are legendary. Whether it is range wars over cattle, sheepherders and cattlemen, or just a neighborly dispute, Americans sometimes squabble over the location of fences. Squabbling over physical fences also finds its parallel in the spiritual realm as well. Just as there are debates and feuds over physical fences, so people have debated and heatedly discussed standards in the Christian life.

If the fence is manmade, then it is quite conceivable that two different men in two different spheres of influence might build two fences in different places, each fence to protect from the same cliff. The question is, what is to be done in such a case? As in all issues of life, the Bible gives the exact answer to these questions of border disputes.

The Apostle Paul, in his Epistle to the Romans, addressed the idea of spiritual border disputes, or fences built in different places. He instructs, "Him that is weak in the faith receive ye, but not to doubtful disputations."[104] Following this instruction are examples of people who took different positions on the same issues and were both right with God. In fact, there may be no other chapter that so completely deals with the questions surrounding cliffs and fences as does Romans 14.

In order to understand the instruction of the passage, it is first necessary to grasp the issues at stake in Paul's illustrations. The first dealt with questions of diet: "For one believeth that he may eat all things: another, who is weak, eateth herbs."[105] As to the exact origins of this problem in Rome, there are unanswered questions. An issue addressed in Paul's First Epistle to the Corinthians may supply some insight into what could have been a similar problem in Rome. To the Corinthians, Paul spoke of limiting one's personal rights so that no one would knowingly cause another to stumble.[106] He spoke of "things offered to idols," and the same may have been the issue for the Roman church. The propensity was for discussion about things where the Scriptures were not always articulate. Roman believers were to receive one another, but not to quarrels based upon human reasoning instead of clear Scripture.

Diet was not the only issue, however. There were also questions about the different feast days and holy days of the Jews: "One man esteemeth one day above another: another esteemeth every day alike."[107] Presumably, some who had been saved out of Judaism might find it difficult to disregard the holy days that, when celebrated according to the Scripture, so clearly pointed to Christ. Others, not having the same background, would simply try to live every day as if their time belonged to God and no day would be any different from any other.

Both issues caused the tendency for believers to argue on matters that were not clearly addressed in Scripture. Accordingly, Paul in his epistle laid out some very clear principles for dealing with differences of opinion.

The first issue that caused controversy was one of diet: whether or not to eat meat. Assuming that the meats had been offered to idols, the cliff to be avoided in this case was one of the Ten Commandments: "Thou shalt have no other gods before me."[108] There may have been some who had been saved out of a life of pagan temple worship who wanted nothing to do with anything that the old temples had to offer, including the meat used in sacrifice. In the analogy of this book, such a person would build his fence a long way from the cliff. Some, in fact, refused to eat any meat, lest they possibly eat something that had been offered in sacrifice to a pagan idol. Those who had their fence a long way back were the weaker brethren. There were others who realized that the meat was not the property of the idol at all, but the property of God who owns everything on the earth, according to Scripture. While there were people who worshiped things that God had made, their worship did not affect His ownership of anything, certainly not the meat offered in sacrifice. Furthermore, the meat was sold in the markets at discounted prices after being used in the pagan ritual. Since devoted men do not offer second-rate gifts to their chosen deity, the meat was usually the best cuts of meat to be had. It only made sense, then, for frugal Christians to go to the market, buy the meat, bring it into their homes, and enjoy it as another means of God's provision for them. Those who did this had their fence built closer to the cliff.

In a local church setting, it would only be a matter of time before the differences would surface and the debates would begin. In order to avoid these debates, the Apostle Paul gave some very important principles for dealing with these and other such disputes.

Before examining the principles given, however, it is first important to insert a caveat. Many today have taken Romans 14 in hand to prove that anyone who insists on a separated stand is ignoring the direct commands of Scripture. They say that if a person insists that certain music is wrong, then he is disregarding Paul's admonition. They assert that the Scriptures do not speak specifically on the issue of dress and so anyone who presumes to tell them specifically what they can and cannot wear is judging his brother. In short, for those who want to be like the world, Romans 14 can be misapplied as justification of their worldliness. This passage is nothing like a license to worldliness, however. Too many deny the existence of the cliff and so see no need for the fence. Paul's instruction to the Roman believers deals with issues based in human reasoning, not in clear-cut Scripture. Music and dress are issues that are indeed dealt with in the Word of God, and there are cliffs to be avoided in both areas. The fences that different churches build are debatable, but too many endeavor to build a fence before they even know the location of the cliff. In the physical realm, such a practice would be disastrous, resulting in death or serious harm. In the spiritual realm it is no different. The principle of knowing where the cliff is will surface from Paul's admonition to the Romans about doubtful issues.

The first principle in dealing with doubtful issues is what might be called the principle of acceptance. It is different for each party depending on where he has built his fence: "Let not him that eateth despise him that eateth not; and let not him which eateth not despise him that eateth."[109] In this case, the one who ate meat had his fence built closer to the edge of the cliff than his brother who refused to eat meat.

The one with greater liberty because of the closer fence would have a tendency to despise his brother. He might want to ask, "Don't you know that the meat, the market, and even the idol itself belong to God? Why don't you just lighten up, get off your high horse, and eat some of this good meat?" (Bear in mind that, although this man was more lenient than his brother, he still was not falling off the cliff by committing idolatry, despite his fence being built close to the cliff.) The word *despise* in this verse means "to show by one's attitude or manner of treatment that an entity has no merit or worth."[110] Paul's command was clear: Do not despise those with higher standards than yours.

The man with the fence farther back from the cliff would have a tendency to judge his brother. His thinking would run something like this: "Doesn't that man know that the meat he eats has been offered in a demonic ritual to a pagan deity? How can he allow that in his home knowing the wickedness that goes on in the pagan temples?" The tendency to judge is apparent. Evidently this tendency to judge was stronger than the tendency to despise because God elaborated a bit on this prohibition: "Who art thou that judgest another man's servant? To his own master he standeth or falleth. Yea, he shall be holden up: for God is able to make him stand."[111] To the man with the more stringent standard, it is difficult to conceive that a person less separated than he can actually be right with God, but God is the One who rightfully judges. God is the Master and every believer just the servant. Just as it would be unjust for someone other than the servant's master to command or judge the servant, so it is wrong for one believer to judge another believer.

In the first example Paul gave, it is noteworthy that human reasoning, using the Word of God as a starting point, could arrive at either position. Both would start from the same Scripture, both reasoning processes would be sound, and yet the two would arrive at very different conclusions. There are times when the disputes among believers are not based upon human reasoning from some passage of Scripture, but on the acceptance or rejection of Bible principles. Such disputes should never be forced into Romans 14 because they do not fit the criteria of the passage. Preservation of this distinction is vital, or the interpreter will begin to "wrest the Scriptures."[112]

Today's Western culture talks a lot about acceptance and tolerance, but it does not really understand either word or concept. When a man stands up and proclaims a definite standard of right and wrong, he is often accused of being intolerant and in need of just accepting people for who they are. This philosophy has come into churches like a tidal wave, often leaving strong Bible preaching as its first casualty. If the Old Testament is a fair sampling of human nature, then strong preaching has always been less than popular. Strong preaching, when done according to the prophets of old, can be very condemnatory to be sure. The difference, however, is one of authority. It is not necessarily true that anyone who tells me I am wrong is judging me. It may be that the man who tells me I am wrong is simply speaking on behalf of the God of heaven, whose right it is to judge all mankind. If a man shows me from the Word of God that what I am doing is wrong, then the judgment that I feel when he speaks does not ultimately come from him but from God. Many are the times when the Holy Spirit judges a man while His human messenger delivers some message. The man can either respond to the Spirit's work in repentance, or he can do away with the human messenger. Too often, mankind chooses to lash out at the visible messenger, instead of dealing with the real problem of conviction. The messenger is not judging anyone, but the God who sent the messenger is. This is an important distinction to remember when looking at the truths of acceptance of those who disagree with one another.

To the principle of acceptance is added the principle of accountability. After mentioning some believers' observance of holy days, Paul added:

> Let every man be fully persuaded in his own mind. He that regardeth the day, regardeth it unto the Lord; and he that regardeth not the day, to the Lord he doth not regard it. He that eateth, eateth to the Lord, for he giveth God thanks; and he that eateth not, to the Lord he eateth not, and giveth God thanks. For none of us liveth to himself, and no man dieth to himself. For whether we live, we live unto the Lord; and whether we die, we die unto the Lord; whether we live therefore, or die, we are the Lord's. For to this end Christ both died, and rose, and revived, that he might be Lord both of the dead and living.[113]

Before any believer sets out to build a fence, he must be certain for himself that the fence he is about to build is in the right place. There must be no doubt in his mind, when he sets his standard. In the final analysis, the believer does what he does not for himself, but for Christ who is his rightful Master and Lord. If he builds a fence a long way from the cliff— has a higher standard—he does so not for selfish reasons, but for spiritual reasons, so that he can best please Christ. Likewise, if he builds his fence close to the cliff, he should do so because he is absolutely convinced that it is right for him to do. Anyone who builds a fence should never do so to please parents, pastors, or peers. He should build the fence to please

Christ alone, who, by virtue of His death and resurrection, is the rightful Lord of all.

Another reason that the believer must be completely convinced is that he will one day have to give a defense of his stand, not before man, but before God Himself.

> But why dost thou judge thy brother? Or why dost thou set at nought thy brother? For we shall all stand before the judgment seat of Christ. For it is written, As I live, saith the Lord, every knee shall bow to me, and every tongue shall confess to God. So then every one of us shall give account of himself to God.[114]

The principle of acceptance is tied to the principle of accountability. It is indeed wrong for a man to judge God's servant, because one day God's servant will give account to God Himself. The reason for being fully persuaded makes perfect sense in the light of every man's accountability to God. Given the information that the New Testament reveals about Christ, the world, and the coming judgment of believers, one might find it helpful to compile some of the information and augment it with "sanctified imagination." One day every believer will stand before Jesus Christ, before whose face the earth and heavens will flee away.[115] There the believer will look into eyes that are as a flame of fire,[116] burning with power and blazing with holiness. He will have to give a narrative of his life, telling what he has done and said.[117] If he has violated the Bible principle of separation from the world, he will be ashamed, finally realizing the full significance of the truth that "friendship with the world is enmity with God."[118] The believer may have to gaze upon the One who gave His last drop of blood to pay for the sins of the world, and explain why he knowingly chose to be His enemy. There will be many Christians, who today scorn the idea of separated living and the whole idea of standards, who will wish on that day that they could go back and implement the very standards that they once scorned. Cliffs and fences become far more important when the principle of accountability affects the discussion. If a man is convinced that he is right with God in what he is doing, then he can persist in doing what he does, realizing that while man does not have the right to judge him, God will judge him one day.

There is one more principle for dealing with disputes found in Romans 14. To the principle of acceptance, based upon the principle of accountability, is added the principle of acquiescence. That is, there are times when one believer may have to live by fences that are not necessarily his own. In determining and building fences, it is important to remember that there are spheres of influence. For instance, there is the home, which represents a father's unique sphere of influence. The father must build fences for his own home, realizing that he will one day give an account before God for his authority.[119] Likewise, the pastor has a sphere of influence that includes and is limited to his own church.[120] There are times, however, when the spheres of influence overlap. For instance, I may take my family to another man's home at his invitation, a home whose fence is farther from the cliff than mine (he has a higher standard in a particular area). While I am in his home, it may be necessary for me to temporarily live within his fence for the purpose of not causing him to stumble. In the words of the Apostle Paul:

> Let us not therefore judge one another any more: but judge this rather, that no man put a stumbling block or an occasion to fall in his brother's way. I know, and am persuaded by the Lord Jesus, that there is nothing unclean of itself: but to him that esteemeth any thing to be unclean, to him it is unclean. But if thy brother be grieved with thy meat, now walkest thou not charitably. Destroy not him with thy meat for whom Christ died.[121]

The words here are important to a proper understanding of Paul's meaning. By *stumbling block*, Paul meant "an opportunity to experience pain (take offence) or make a misstep."[122] Paul was saying that it is possible for a man by his actions to cause another man to sin. While this cannot always be anticipated, there are times when one can predict what will and what will not cause others to fall. Rather than judge other believers' actions, the believer is to devote the same energy to predicting what might cause others to fall. Another word that Paul used is more familiar to modern English: the Greek word *skandalon*. Its meaning in Paul's day was "an action or circumstance that leads one to act contrary to a proper course of action or set of beliefs."[123] The two terms refer to the same kinds of things.

In the analogy of cliffs and fences, it is quite conceivable for a man to have his fence built a long way from the cliff because he is weak in that particular area. For another brother to flaunt his liberty before the weaker brother might cause the weaker brother to fall into sin. In order to prevent such an occurrence from happening, it will be necessary for the stronger brother to acquiesce temporarily to the fence of the weaker brother, particularly while in the weaker brother's sphere of influence. If there is not acquiescence, then the good that the one brother might try to do (buy discounted meat, for example) might be misunderstood and slandered. A man is to consider the consequences of his actions on others before he acts. Failure to do so would violate Paul's summarizing command, "Let not then your good be evil spoken of."[124]

In reality, the most important elements in life are not the fences built to keep us from the cliffs. Christianity is not essentially a list of issues about which to quarrel with others. Paul makes it clear: "For the kingdom of God is not meat and drink; but righteousness, peace, and joy in the Holy Ghost."[125] If another person in his own sphere of influence has a fence built in a different place, it should not be a problem. The essence of Christianity is not any one issue, but rather a relationship. First of all, Christianity is righteousness, or being right with God. Secondly, it is peace, or being right with man. Finally, it is joy in the Holy Ghost, simply enjoying the life and freedom that Christ has made possible.

In the final analysis, it is right to build fences. It is necessary to set standards. Whenever those standards conflict with those of another believer, however, it is paramount that the child of God first ensure that he himself is right with God, and then right with his fellow man according to the principles laid out in the Word of God. Having secured both relationships, he should then rejoice in all that God has done for him, differences of opinion with Christians notwithstanding. Border differences should never become heated disputes in Christianity.

CHAPTER 9:
FENCE PHOTOS

A word fitly spoken is like apples of gold in pictures of silver.
Proverbs 25:11

The Chinese are reputed to have a proverb that states, "A picture is worth a thousand words." While there are no drawings or photographs in this book, illustrations of specifics may serve to further flesh out the principles of acceptance, accountability, and acquiescence laid out in the previous chapter.

In order to illustrate the concepts of Romans 14, I have decided to include some personal examples of some fences that I have in place for my family, my particular sphere of influence. Before looking at the fence, it is important to first identify the cliffs that are to be avoided. First, there is the cliff of visual purity: "I will set no wicked thing before mine eyes."[126] Second, there is the cliff of properly used time: "Redeeming the time because the days are evil."[127] These two cliffs are non-negotiable if I want to be right with God. In order to avoid these two cliffs, I have erected a fence in my life: no television in the home. There are times when we watch DVDs on our computer, but I do not have a television capable of receiving broadcasts or cable. The reason is that I am weak in the area of controlling the TV. If I had a television, I fear that I would not keep myself from seeing wicked things. One problem is that often the only way I know that something is offensive is to see it. By the time I have seen the offensive material and passed judgment upon it, I have allowed a wicked thing before my eyes. While I could go to great lengths to study what others say about a particular program, I am afraid that I would not do so because of the time involved. If my entertainment becomes so much time-consuming work, then there is a point at which it ceases to be worth the trouble to me. While there are electronic devices that filter out offensive content, I am afraid of the temptation to watch something that interests me, but does not have the closed captioning necessary for the electronic device to filter out the filth. For me, the temptation is great.

Another problem with broadcast television is that it can be so endless. One show follows another in rapid succession and before long, I have taken opportunities that I had to serve God with my time and squandered them on worthless, time-wasting TV shows. So I try to solve both problems by not owning a TV. Admittedly, my fence is a long way back from the cliff. You may have no problem controlling the TV because you carefully use the information that is available to you to screen shows before you ever allow them into your home. You may employ the devices available to protect you from offensive scenes and language, disciplining your watching to only those shows that can be controlled by the technology. You may also set strict limits on the amount of time you spend in front of the TV and are very careful to not squander opportunities. Your fence is closer to the cliff, but that does not mean you have fallen over it. Our fences for the same cliffs are built in different places.

Now you know where my fence is and that it is built in a different place from yours. The first principle of border disputes is that of acceptance. I, the weaker brother, am not to judge you in this matter. Likewise, you are not to despise me. You could keep a television in your home all your life and still live a life pleasing to God. Conversely, I could still set wicked things before my eyes and waste time, even though I don't have a television. The essential matter is that our fellowship with God and each other not be broken over the issue. Your reasoning was sound in arriving at your conclusion, as was mine. Therefore arguing about the issue would be an argument based upon human reasoning and not on the Word of God. We are both to accept each other and respect each other's positions, despite the fact that both are different.

The principle of accountability comes into play as well. I should not refuse a TV in my home because I heard of someone else who holds the same standard. I should not flaunt my standard before others so that they will somehow think me more spiritual than anyone else. Indeed, if I lived my entire life and never told anyone that I did not have a TV, I would be far less tempted to be a Pharisee in regard to my standard. The only reason I should build the no-TV fence should be because I am fully persuaded that this is the best course of action to take before God my Judge. Likewise, you are fully free to own and watch a television, but you must understand that you will one day give an account to God for everything that you have seen while watching it. If, after considering the cliffs from Scripture, you are fully convinced that you can own and watch a television and defend that decision before the throne of God, then get yourself a TV. If, however, there is some doubt in your mind, then you are condemned in whatever doubtful practice you allow. Paul put it this way: "Happy is he that condemneth not himself in that thing which he alloweth. And he that doubteth is damned if he eat, because he eateth not of faith: for whatsoever is not of faith is sin."[128]

Let us assume in this illustration that we have found out about each other's different fences and that we are still friends. In the course of time, you decide to have my family over to your house for a meal one Friday evening. I would be entering a sphere of influence that is not my own by coming to your house. Since you know about my fence ahead of time, you should probably insist that the television not be turned on the entire time I am in your home. That way, you could be sure that you did not do anything that would cause me to violate my conscience and stumble. In this case, you have temporarily acquiesced to my standard in order not to offend me or to make me weaker.

I, on the other hand, should be careful not to judge you when I walk into your house and see the television sitting in your home. Should someone in your home forget about my standard and turn the TV on, I am not to suddenly end our friendship, storm out of your house, and write you off as a wicked compromiser. Either I could request politely that we spend our time together doing something else, or I could choose not to even bring up the differences between our standards. In both your actions and mine, there should be an attitude of acquiescence.

In the illustration, all three principles of differing fences are present: acceptance, accountability, and acquiescence. The point is that we never allow things of this nature to rob us of the fellowship that we ought to enjoy as believers. Paul admonished:

Let us therefore follow after the things which make for peace, and things wherewith one may edify another. For meat destroy not the work of God. All things indeed are pure; but it is evil for that man who eateth with offense. It is good neither to eat flesh, nor to drink wine, nor any thing whereby thy brother stumbleth, or is offended, or is made weak.[129]

When the focus becomes the edification of the other believer and not the error of his position and the correctness of mine, then believers more accurately reflect the Christ whom they ought to serve. Cliffs and fences are important, but never should they get in the way of serving Him and edifying one another.

CHAPTER 10:
NURSERY GATES

Remove not the ancient landmark, which thy fathers have set.
Proverbs 22:28

Many nurseries have them. They are put in place so that the young detainees will not escape their interment and wander at large into auditoriums, parking lots, bathrooms, or other places ill-suited for toddlers. They are special fences that are easily enough breached or cleared by an older child or adult, but quite effective at keeping toddlers in an area that is safe. The toddler cannot begin to imagine the power of an automobile, even if it were explained to him; nor can he begin to fathom the danger of sticking his head in the toilet or going against the flow of an oncoming crowd. There is no way that any nursery worker can ever explain the reason for the confines of the nursery to a toddler because he is simply too young to comprehend the full import of the situation and the reason for the gate.

When it comes to cliffs and fences in the spiritual realm, there are times when a certain maturity level is necessary to even be able to perceive the cliff that exists. Just as a toddler cannot comprehend all the dangers that await him beyond the nursery gate, so young Christians and young people, for that matter, are sometimes simply incapable of comprehending the cliff that exists beyond a certain fence. In such cases, it is not only necessary, but also Biblically correct to adopt the fence of an authority until the person under authority grows to greater maturity. The writer of Hebrews says it this way, "Remember them which have the rule over you, who have spoken unto you the word of God: whose faith follow, considering the end of their conversation."[130] While mimicking a leader's trust in God is certainly included in this admonition, the word *faith* seems to go beyond their acceptance of God's Word in this passage. Their faith includes areas of life that affect their lifestyle so much that the lifestyle and the end of it is given as a reason for following the leader's faith. This would include a lot of corollaries that exist because of the leader's trust in God, including the fences that he has built. While this application does not remove the truth of being fully persuaded in one's own mind, it does allow for the development of that mind along God's guidelines. The leader is more mature than his followers and knows more of the cliffs that exist in life. He has grown to the point where he fully understands those cliffs and, knowing the dangers if he were to fall off them, he has built fences. Those who follow him are to imitate his walk with God considering that one day, assuming the leader remains faithful, the end of his lifestyle will be blessed of God.

When my family was at the Grand Canyon, there were many times when my three-year-old son could not see the reason for the fence. The ground on the other side of the fence sloped slightly up to where his short body and its accompanying visual perspective could not perceive the cliff just beyond the chain link fence that had been built. This circumstance was neither his fault, nor was it my fault, nor were those who built the fence to blame; it was simply a reality of life that he had not grown to the place to where he could see the reason for the fence. In his case, he simply had to trust the leadership, his father in this case, to dictate to him where he could and couldn't walk. The fence kept him safe, even though he could never understand fully the reason why. So it is in the spiritual realm, that followers should sometimes adopt the fences of leaders until they have matured to the place where they can see the cliff.

Several examples come immediately to mind. Any father who walks with God will desire to keep his children from certain worldly influences that exist around them. He will see the cliffs that present a danger for his family and will work to construct fences to keep them from the danger. It is impossible for a teenager who has never been sexually active to fully comprehend the full mental and emotional ramifications of the sexual union between man and woman, much less the power of sexual temptation. There will probably be no way that such a young person will be able to understand the purpose for a fence that his father has put in place in an effort to keep the youth from temptation. Young ladies tend to have bad track records when it comes to choosing men in their lives, especially when they are completely void of parental input and veto power. The reason is that maturity can spot problems that adolescence cannot see. Caring adults will erect fences that many times the young person will not fully comprehend. The same principle applies to young people in a school, be it Christian high school or Christian college. Even college students cannot fully see the dangers that lie in wait for them, and so find it necessary to be given boundaries, fences, within which to live. For a time after the young person leaves the home or institution, it is perfectly permissible and acceptable for him to live by the fences that restricted him when he was under someone else's authority.

The problem comes when the person does not personalize the fences. In order to personalize the fence, he must first fully comprehend the cliff. Comprehending the cliff does not necessarily mean falling off the cliff and suffering the consequences of the fall, but it does entail growing to the point where a man can at least see over the edge from behind the fence. Until a man has grown to the point where he can see over the cliff from behind the fence, he is by no means ready to tear down the fence and construct another. Once he is to the point where he can see over the edge of the cliff and ascertain a little of the reasons for which the fence was originally erected, he may then, after being fully persuaded in his own mind, remove the fence for himself and construct another in a different place. If the person is lazy and never grows to the place where he can see the reason for the fence, he will flounder through life and most likely end up moving the fence and maybe even disregarding the idea of fences altogether. The problem was not the existence of a fence in his adolescence, although the person who built the fence often gets the blame. The problem is one of retardation: the person never grew to the place where he could see the cliff and then construct his own protective fence. A mentally retarded person is always a tragedy, especially when the physical growth is a great many years ahead of the mental development. Still sadder, however, is spiritual retardation, a common problem even in the first century Church. The writer of Hebrews spoke of it in this way:

> Of [Christ] we have many things to say, and hard to be uttered, seeing ye are dull of hearing. For when for the time ye ought to

be teachers, ye have need that one teach you again which be the first principles of the oracles of God; and are become such as have need of milk, and not of strong meat. For every one that useth milk is unskillful in the word of righteousness: for he is a babe. But strong meat belongeth to them that are of full age, even those who by reason of use have their senses exercised to discern both good and evil.[131]

The passing of time should have brought the Hebrew Christians to a greater place of maturity in their lives, just as time brings growth in a child's body. They were retarded, however. The time that should have yielded maturity had been squandered and the Hebrew Christians were still "babes" spiritually. The problem also existed in the Corinthian church,[132] and continues to this day in the lives of many Christians.

It is part of human nature for a man to assume that he is more mature than he really is. The toddler assumes that he can run down a steep hill and, assaying to do so, plows the hill with his nose. The seventeen-year-old driver assumes that he is adroit in handling a vehicle, yet, as any insurance company will verify, is far more prone to accidents than more seasoned, experienced motorists. Likewise immature men and women like to assume that they are more spiritually mature than they are and begin to question, if not chafe under, the standards imposed upon them. Indeed, questions they ask are sometimes very necessary to the maturation process, but some questions are posed with the assumption that they are unanswerable. Any answer given has already been deemed to be unsatisfactory before it is even heard. Such attitudes reveal the maturity level of the individual and consequently, his inability to see cliffs or remove fences.

Many teachable Christians have gone through the very process being described. They came up under certain standards, at times not fully understanding them, but accepting them because an authority had put them in place. As time went on, they matured in Christ to the place where, one by one, they saw the cliffs that the standards of their youth had been erected to avoid. Clearly seeing the cliff caused them to build similar fences in their own lives, having been fully persuaded in their own minds of both the danger of the cliff and the right place to build a fence. As time went on, they looked back to their childhood and realized the great similarity between the fences with which they lived as youngsters and the fences that they themselves have built today. Just as the development of an infant into an adult human being takes time, so this process of spiritual maturity takes time. As with so many areas of the Christian life, there is balance in this area as well. On the one hand, there is nothing wrong with a young person holding a standard because his authority holds that standard. On the other hand, for that young person, as he matures, to never progress to the place where he sees the cliff and builds his own fence is a great spiritual tragedy.

SECTION II:
SOME SPECIFIC ISSUES

CHAPTER 11:
CHRISTIAN CLOTHING

Having dealt with the idea of forming standards, I will now move on to certain issues. It will not be my purpose to dictate standards to readers, but rather to go to the Scripture and clearly define some cliffs that exist in certain areas that are sometimes controversial today. Each chapter will deal with a different issue.

The subject of what to wear and what not to wear is a controversial issue and has been for many years. In fact, it was the issue of dress that first got me to thinking about standards in general, many years ago. The debates over dress usually do not include men's dress much, if at all.[133] Rather, they focus on women's dress standards. What can the ladies wear and what can they not wear, and where should the line be drawn? This is most often the core of the debate whenever someone mentions the subject of dress.

The first Bible principle of dress concerns not just the women, but both sexes. It is found not far from the battlement principle in Deuteronomy: "The woman shall not wear that which pertaineth unto a man, neither shall a man put on a woman's garment: for all that do so are an abomination unto the LORD thy God."[134] The Bible principle is that there should be a consistent distinction between the dress of men and women. God hates the unisex movement. Whenever the Christian removes the distinction between man and woman, he has fallen off the cliff and sinned against God.

Often, this verse becomes the sole basis for one standard, namely, that women should never wear pants. It is certainly valid for a woman to build a "no pants" fence to keep herself from this cliff. It is important to remember some things about this verse, however. First of all, pants were not an issue when God gave the law to Moses. At the time, both sexes wore tunics. Second of all, the principle can be applied to far more articles of clothing than just pants. For example, there was a day when Christian ladies did not wear baseball caps because a cap definitely pertained to a man. Too often, this verse is used to support the idea that "witches wear britches" as if that were its only purpose in God's Word. In reality, the verse is much broader than just pants on women. Thirdly, it is important to remember that the verse addresses men's apparel as well as women's apparel. It is at this point that some great inconsistencies emerge.

When I was only a junior-aged camper, I attended a Christian camp that took a strong stand against women wearing pants. Being a boy, I was completely unaffected by the standard and could not have cared less what the girls wore. They, as all of us boys knew at the time, were so thoroughly infested with cooties and other dangerous maladies that we never gave them a second thought. I do remember, however, a skit that was performed at the camp. The skit consisted of men counselors dressing up in skirts and dresses and acting like cheerleaders. If I remember correctly, they even wore makeup. I remember being uncomfortable with the skit. My discomfort could have come from the fact that the skit was not funny to me—a grievous sin, in my way of thinking—or it could have come from the fact that what the men were doing was wrong before God. While I do not know the basis for my discomfort at the time, I do know that what those men did that day was wrong before God. Looking back on it, the glaring inconsistency strikes me hardest of all. Women were not allowed to wear pants because they pertained to a man, but men wore women's garments to make others laugh. If I noticed the inconsistency, I am sure that there were teenagers at the same camp who noticed the inconsistency as well. When the authority takes part of a verse of Scripture, forms a high standard based upon that verse, and then ignores the rest of the verse from which the standard came, he is asking for rebellion in the hearts of those under his influence.

To the principle of distinction between the sexes can be added the Bible principle of covering. The New Testament further develops this principle for the women. At the risk of being redundant, suffice it to say that God equates the exposure of the thighs, of both men and women, with nakedness.[135] Outside the privacy of marriage, nakedness is always a shameful thing. God is the One who created clothing to cover the shame of man's sin, and man is to remain covered because of his sin.[136]

The New Testament deals more specifically than the Old Testament with the principles of women's modesty and gives some clear principles for dress. Before any person can set standards of dress in his or her sphere of influence, it is essential to understand these principles. In his First Epistle to Timothy, the Apostle Paul gave his young protégé a manual by which the New Testament church was to be run. Part of this manual dealt with women's dress standards:

> In like manner also, that women adorn themselves in modest apparel, with shamefacedness and sobriety; not with broided hair, or gold, or pearls, or costly array; But (which becometh women professing godliness) with good works.[137]

The woman is to add these character qualities to her modest apparel: shamefacedness, sobriety, and good works. A definition of each of these terms is essential to understanding the principles God has for women's dress.

Modern English readers find the Greek word here translated "modest" to be a familiar word. Coming from this Greek word is the modern English word *cosmetic*. There are many different New Testament words that are related to this word, with both good and bad connotations. Regardless of whether the related word is used in a good or bad sense, the idea of order is always present. This particular word in relation to women's apparel means "well-arranged, seemly, modest."[138] In addition to describing a woman's dress, it is also used in the list of character qualities essential in a pastor, being translated by the phrase *of good behavior*.[139] God wants a woman's dress to be orderly and in accordance with good taste. For a woman to clash or wear "loud" clothing simply to draw attention to herself is immodest in the sight of God. Although not an expert on women's fashions, I have seen pictures of fashions in different malls from time to time that clearly violate this Bible principle. While the models wearing the clothing have been properly covered, the clothes that covered them were so outlandish that they were immodest. As a believer begins to create standards for dress, it is important to understand that a woman's dress must always be orderly.

Orderliness is not sufficient by itself, however. It is possible for a woman's clothing to be well-ordered and yet be improper before God. To the idea of orderliness, Paul also added the concept of shamefacedness. The word means "a sense of *shame, modesty...reverence.*"[140] A woman's dress should show reverence, first to the God who designed and owns her, and second to the male authority (father or husband) that God has put in her life. There is a widely used concept of shame in the Scripture that is not quite the same as the concept used here in relation to a woman's dress.

Accordingly, [shamefacedness] is prominently objective in its reference, having regard to others; while [shame] is subjective, making reference to oneself and one's actions. It is often said that [shamefacedness] precedes and prevents the shameful act, [shame] reflects upon its consequences in the *shame* it brings with it' [sic] (Cope, Aristotle, rhet. 5, 6, 1). [Shamefacedness] is the nobler word, [shame] the stronger; while "[shamefacedness] would always restrain a good man from an unworthy act, [shame] would sometimes restrain a bad one." (Note: The original used Greek words, which have been replaced by their English equivalent in brackets.) (Trench, sections 19, 20)[141]

The basis of shamefacedness, with regard to women's dress, is the recognition of the fact that God designed a woman's body for her husband alone. Anywhere outside of the marriage bedroom, the woman is to have her body covered properly so as to not advertise her sexual availability. Shamefacedness recognizes that a woman's body in general is never to be on public display, and that certain parts of her body in particular are more sexually attractive than others.[142] Accordingly, a godly woman wears clothes that cover her body and do not advertise her more attractive parts. She understands that it is possible for her to dress in such a way that men would be tempted to lust after her, in violation of the Word of God. The woman who dresses modestly with shamefacedness looks at the consequences of her wearing something before she ever puts it on to go out in public.

The issue of standards becomes very important at this juncture of the discussion on women's dress. In order for a woman to understand shamefacedness, she must be instructed, either by a male authority figure (preferably her father) or by a godly woman who has been previously instructed by a male authority in her own life. The man understands the way that other men will look at his wife or daughter when she wears a certain thing, while most women either do not comprehend or else do not fully realize the effect that a certain garment may have upon a man. On the one hand, there are men so vile that they will lust after a woman regardless of how modestly she is dressed. On the other hand, it is possible for a woman to cause a man to sin by improperly exposing her body. (The sin need not be physical to still be sin. A covetous, lustful look is a violation of the tenth commandment and is just as much a sin as rape is in God's eyes.) The need for godly male leadership in this regard cannot be stressed too strongly.

In addition to modesty with shamefacedness, it is also necessary for the woman to include the character quality of sobriety. Sobriety emphasizes the aspect of self-control in a woman's apparel.[143] There has always been a temptation for women to spend large amounts of time and money on fashions, both clothing and accessories. The Apostle Paul wanted women to know that they must exercise self-control in their efforts to beautify the external person. He says that they are to be adorned "not with broided hair, or gold, or pearls, or costly array."[144] He is not necessarily saying that it is wrong for a woman to ever have some kind of ornamental hairdo or to ever wear some gold necklace or pearl earrings. He is saying that a woman should exercise self-control in these areas. A woman who spends hours in front of a mirror but only minutes reading her Bible is grossly lacking in godly self-control.

Sometimes Christians get the idea that sensuality is the opposite of modesty. In reality, drawing attention to self is the opposite of modesty. A woman can draw attention to self in many different ways, three of which Paul addressed in his letter to Timothy. It is common to hear that sensual clothing is immodest, but so is "loud" clothing that clashes. The same is true for lavish clothing that draws attention to self. If a woman were to wear clashing clothing, she would be saying, "Look at me; I am weird." If she were to wear sensual clothing, she would be saying, "Look at me; I am available." If she were to wear lavish clothing, she would be saying, "Look at me; I am rich." All three are wrong because all three draw attention to self. God does not want the attention to be put on self, but rather on Him. It is possible for a woman to dress and act in such a way as to draw attention to God, instead of self. The woman's life points to someone, either herself or her Lord. God wants her to direct the attention to her Lord. In his discussion on modesty, the Apostle Paul tells how a woman can best point to her Lord.

The final trait that should accompany a woman's modest apparel should be good works. God is primarily concerned with the inward person. In the midst of a society that worships the external, God wants to see special emphasis on the woman inside. Peter conveyed the same idea when he wrote concerning Christian wives:

Whose adorning let it not be that outward adorning of plaiting the hair, and of wearing of gold, or of putting on of apparel; But let it be the hidden man of the heart, in that which is not corruptible, even the ornament of a meek and quiet spirit, which is in the sight of God of great price.[145]

The Bible principles for a woman's dress go beyond the mere externals, although externals are important. Whenever Bible writers spoke of women's dress in the New Testament, it was never long before they got around to the subject of the woman's heart. No discussion of women's standards can be complete without stressing the need for positive inward godliness from the woman.

To summarize, the Bible lays out the following principles for women's dress:

- Distinction of the sexes, Deuteronomy 22:5
- Covered thighs, Isaiah 47:1–3
- Modest, orderly apparel, 1 Timothy 2:9
- Respect for God and her male authority, 1 Timothy 2:9
- Self-discipline with regard to the externals, 1 Timothy 2:9–10
- Good works as a distinguishing characteristic, 1 Timothy 2:10

These principles are not just my opinion or the opinion of some other preacher somewhere; they are nonnegotiable cliffs set up by God Himself. If the woman violates these, she has sinned against the Lord who saved her soul. Having seen these cliffs, it will be necessary for the reader to construct fences, or formulate standards, for his or her sphere of influence. He will have to determine where he stands about women wearing ball caps, pants, overalls, etc. He will have to decide for himself what constitutes disorderly apparel. He will have to set boundaries for what is too tight, too low, and too short. He will have to define what is too lavish externally and what is appropriate. The standards are issues for which he will one day give account before God Himself.

A couple of years ago, my family and I were in a restaurant in northern Virginia. At the same restaurant sat a group of teenagers who attracted my attention. To be sure, there are young people who attract my attention from time to time because they are so odious in their manners, conversation, and overall behavior, but these young people were much different. They were anything but prudish—their corporate laughter became hearty and loud from time to time—but there was something about them that was conspicuous. They all wore stylish clothing that was quite plainly in touch with the latest fashions, but the latest fashions had been modified a bit on each young person there. The young ladies wore tops that adequately covered them, were a little looser than others around them, and tastefully coordinated with the rest of their attire. They looked sharp and wholesome, yet stylish on the outside. Their conversation, too, seemed to match their clothing. They laughed and talked of embarrassing things that had befallen some of them in the course of the past week, but the crudeness and vulgarity so often characteristic of young people were conspicuous by their absence. After observing them for the better part of an hour, I finally approached them and asked them to tell me a little bit about themselves. They responded that they were all members of an independent Baptist church. In fact, they were all planning to go to church after their meal. Coincidentally, I was planning to attend the same church of which they were all members that night. I went away from that encounter thanking God for the difference that a right exterior can make in communicating the testimony of Christ.

CHAPTER 12:
MORALITY IN MUSIC

O ne of the most divisive issues in the United States today is the area of music in general, and Christian music in particular. There are some who assert that the Bible says nothing about what music is appropriate and inappropriate. There are others who are quite strict in their music standards. Those who are strict often assert that those who disagree with them have ignored Bible principles that relate to music, while those that insist that there are no Bible principles relating to musical styles see anyone else as legalists.

The central issue with respect to music is rarely, if ever, the lyrics of songs. It is difficult to justify the lyrics of a rap that advocates murder or the lyrics of a country and western song that advocates adultery. The debate over music instead finds its battlefield in the music style itself, totally devoid of the words. If there is such a thing as immorality in the musical style itself, then the Bible can speak to musical styles. If there is not a definite immorality in music, then all who insist upon music standards are legalists.

Music is a form of art. When most people think of art, they probably think primarily of the visual arts, such as painting, photography, or sculpture. Music, however, is just as much art as are any of the visual media. It is audio art instead of visual art. This is an important concept to realize because the Bible has nothing to say about most of the arts that Westerners enjoy today. For example, one will never find any Bible allusion to motion pictures. To say that the Bible contains no principles that can govern a Christian with respect to his choices of motion pictures, however, is to ignore much of the teaching of Scripture. Once the child of God gets over the fact that his favorite art form is probably not even mentioned by name in the Word of God, he can then proceed to search the Scripture for principles governing his particular choices. For example, God never once mentions photography in the Bible, but He does say, "Whosoever looketh upon a woman to lust after her hath committed adultery with her already in his heart."[146] There are photographs today that are staged, produced, and printed with the express purpose of causing men to lust. In fact, the name given to such visual "art" is quite in keeping with God's standard. These pictures are called pornography, a combination of two transliterated Greek words meaning "fornication" and "writing." Thus, the name itself tells God's opinion on the issue: written fornication. It is no stretch at all to say that if God is against fornication, then He must be against pornography. By this process of reasoning, the modern Christian can take issues about which the Bible does not speak directly, such as photography, and determine a Bible principle on which to build standards regarding that issue.

Whenever anyone evaluates any aspect of art, it is important to realize that the individual building blocks of the art have no morality in and of themselves. For instance, some have taken in hand to demonstrate the amorality of music by playing a single note on a piano and asking the audience if the note was moral or immoral. The proper response is that a single note is neither moral nor immoral; it is amoral. The amoral components of art, however, can be combined in such a way that a work can have morality, or lack thereof. To be consistent, what is true of the audio arts must also be true of the visual arts. I might draw a line on a white sheet of paper and ask a crowd, "Is this line moral or immoral?" The correct response would be that the line has neither morality nor immorality: it is amoral. There would come a time, however, when lines could be combined in such a way that the resulting picture could have definite potential for immorality. As it is with the visual arts, so it is with the audio arts. While the individual notes have no morality of themselves, there comes a time when the right combination of notes and rhythms can produce something with potential for immorality, if there is such a thing as immoral music.

And there is such a thing as immoral music, according to secular observers, authors, and performers. The very name "rock 'n roll" is a case in point. Although a Cleveland, Ohio, disc jockey was first credited with applying the term to a particular style of music, the term had been in use for some time in the lyrics of different songs. The term itself referred to sexual intercourse much, if not all, of the time.[147] Rock musicians have been candid in speaking of the genre's appeal to sexual immorality and Satanic roots. For example, David Bowie, ranked thirty-ninth in the *Rolling Stone* list of the 100 greatest rock artists of all time,[148] had this to say about rock: "Rock has always been the Devil's music. ... I believe rock and roll is dangerous. ... I feel we're only heralding something even darker than ourselves."[149] Michael Jackson, an artist who was criticized for his graphic sexual gestures during his concerts, was asked about these objectionable gestures in a televised interview with Oprah Winfrey. His answer was this: "It happens subliminally. It's the music that compels me to do it. You don't think about it, it just happens. I'm slave to the rhythm."[150] Chicago University professor Allan Bloom observed, "Rock music has one appeal only, a barbaric appeal, to sexual desire—not love, not eros, but sexual desire undeveloped and untutored."[151] The list of secular observers who concur with these analyses could be multiplied. Suffice it to say that the secular world sees rock music as a style at odds with Christianity as set forth in the Word of God.

The purpose of this chapter, however, is not to give a history of rock music and all of the offspring that have come from its original roots. Rock music today has a worldwide appeal, despite its inauguration with English-speaking audiences. I personally have been in ethnic restaurants in the United States that played a blend of their ethnic music and rock. I have heard Chinese rock music and Latin rock music. The reason for this influence is that the wicked flesh of man[152] (including illicit sexual desires, violent desires, materialistic desires, and so forth) is universal. Regardless of man's culture, he still lives with the ungodly desires of the flesh that are contrary to the will of God.[153] It comes as no surprise, then, that the artistic musical expression of unbridled lust comes to influence so many different styles of music. While it is arguably no great loss when rock mixes with the ethnic sounds of the world, the mixing of Christian music with rock is a great tragedy, according to some. In fact, among professing Christians in the United States, there is a tremendous debate over the issue of church music, especially music that has had definite rock influence often going by the abbreviation CCM.[154]

The debate rises or falls on this issue: the potential for immorality in music. If there is such a thing as immoral music, then CCM is wrong. If there is no such thing as immoral music, then any who stand against music are legalists. From time to time, I hear the arguments of people who disagree with the opinions of David Bowie, Michael Jackson, Allan Bloom, and other secular artists and analysts. They usually deny that rock is always fleshly in its appeal. To be sure, rock is not always sexual. Sometimes it is Satanic, other times it is violent, while other times it is rebellious. Anyone who argues that rock is sometimes good must answer the question: Is it possible that so many who were influential in creating rock music can be so wrong about its essence? Could it be that David Bowie really doesn't know rock music? Is Michael Jackson really a pop music neophyte? Or were these men right when they candidly spoke of the music they themselves had created? Since the men and women who invented rock say that it is immoral, I find it difficult to argue with them. To try to prove anything else seems to be a fool's errand.

Many who advocate mixing rock music with Christian lyrics point out that traditional hymns often borrowed music from the current music of the day. Handel, Mendelssohn, and even Chopin, to name a few, have provided the musical setting for hymns. There is no difference, say those who advocate CCM, between borrowing the music of Mendelssohn and borrowing the sound of U2. Both sounds were originally secular and became sacred only by the marriage of Christian lyrics to the secular sound. In order to answer this argument, it is helpful once again to compare music to the visual arts. It is entirely possible to paint a picture that has no moral quality or immoral offensiveness. A landscape would be an example of a picture that is amoral. Many Baptist churches have landscape paintings behind their baptistries, no doubt to remind them of earlier ministries that baptized in the open air. Such a picture has neither a moral nor immoral quality. It is decent insomuch as it reflects the reality of nature, which was ultimately the product of God's creative mind. Similarly, it is possible for a song to be neutral, even amoral. There is no problem with taking such a song and marrying it to Christian words. The problem comes when the music itself is designed to evoke a fleshly response. Such music is completely inappropriate in the worship of God, for "they that worship Him must worship Him in spirit and in truth."[155] There is no room for fleshly worship because the flesh and spirit are at continual enmity. So the argument comparing the practice of borrowing the classics of yesteryear and borrowing the rock songs of today fails because it is an unequal comparison.

In the plethora of material that emerges in the music debate, there is one Bible principle that I have never before seen in print that clearly applies to the area of music. In the New Testament books of history, there are numerous stories of demon possession. The symptoms of demon possession are varied, indeed, but they always included the person's complete loss of control from time to time so that the words that came from his mouth originated with the demon inside instead of with the person. When the demon took control, however, it was over much more that just a person's speech. For example, during the ministry of Jesus, one man brought his demon-possessed boy to Jesus to be healed. The desperate father described the son's symptoms to Jesus: "Ofttimes it hath cast him into the fire, and into the water, to destroy him."[156] Jesus' earthly ministry was characterized by liberating people from demon possession. The most interesting thing to note is what the demons said when they encountered the Son of God during His earthly ministry. For example, Mark recorded this fact about Jesus early on in his gospel: "And he healed many that were sick of divers diseases, and cast out many devils; and suffered not the devils to speak. ..."[157] It should come as no surprise that our Lord would want to silence the word of a demon. The demon works for Satan, the father of lies.[158] One can only imagine the lies that the demon would tell should it be allowed to speak in the presence of Jesus and impressionable bystanders. It only makes perfect sense to tell the demon to hold his tongue. The rest of the verse, however, casts doubt on the interpretation that has just been advanced. The entire sentence says, "He healed many that were sick of divers diseases, and cast out many devils; and suffered not the devils to speak, *because they knew him.*"[159] It would seem that the demons were not telling lies about the Savior at all, but were telling the truth about Him. From this one verse, it might be difficult to assert their veracity unequivocally, but it certainly seems that the demons were not speaking lies. Regardless of what they were saying, God in the flesh disallowed their speech.

There is more than one mention of this silencing behavior when demons were wont to speak, however. Luke records a similar instance to that of Mark: "And devils also came out of many, crying out, and saying, Thou art Christ the Son of God. And he rebuking them suffered them not to speak: for they knew that he was Christ."[160] It comes as no surprise that Jesus is recorded once again to have silenced the demon. What is of interest, however, is the fact that Luke records at least some of the contents of what the demons said before they came out of the humans that they had previously possessed. A quick doctrinal analysis of the demon's assertion reveals it to be orthodox. In every sense of the word, the One casting them out was indeed Christ, the Son of God. No doctrine can be called Christianity that denies this truth. Strange it is, however, that the Son of God did not allow these demons to speak the truth about Him.

Mark gives what might be called a more complete doctrinal statement from the mouth of a demon that is in keeping with the emerging pattern:

> And there was in their synagogue a man with an unclean spirit; and he cried out, Saying, Let us alone; what have we to do with thee, thou Jesus of Nazareth? Art thou come to destroy us? I know thee who thou art, the Holy One of God. And Jesus rebuked him, saying, Hold thy peace, and come out of him.[161]

The scenario was probably different from the previous ones here related in only one respect: the person was not the same person. In all other particulars, the story is the same. As before, this story includes a person whose body had been possessed by a demon. As before, this demon took possession of the person's faculties of speech and began to cry. As before, the things that the demon said had to do with the person of Jesus Christ. This doctrinal statement is interesting because it is more complete than the one in Luke. First of all, this demon asked, "What have we to do with thee, thou Jesus of Nazareth?" This question implies that there is a natural enmity between demons and Jesus Christ. Such an implication is completely true and has been since Satan fell from heaven, presumably before the creation of man. There was certainly nothing misleading about the first part of this demon's statement. Secondly, the demon asked, "Art thou come to destroy us?" Again, this question implies some doctrine. The implication is that Jesus would one day destroy the kingdom of darkness, including this demon and all the other demons that served Satan. Such an implication is true in every way. There will indeed come a time when Satan and all his demons will suffer ultimate and final defeat at the hands of Jesus Christ. There is certainly no fault in this part of the demon's doctrinal statement. Finally, the demon alleged, "I know thee who thou art, the holy one of God." This demon has moved from implying truth through questions to asserting truth through direct statement. Its statement is doctrinally flawless. Indeed, this One standing before them was the Holy One of God.

This doctrinal statement notwithstanding, we would expect the Nazarene to silence the demon as He did in the previous two passages. In fact, the first words out of His mouth had nothing to do with casting the demon out. The first thing He said was, "Hold thy peace." Admittedly, He could have said the entire phrase in one breath, but it is significant that He once again forbade this demon to disseminate the truth about who He was.

After the Son of God arose into heaven, the Holy Spirit came down and multiplied the efforts of Christ by indwelling all believers. From its humble confines in the upper room, the Gospel spread all over the Mediterranean in a matter of just a few years. Before long, the Apostle Paul was led of the Spirit to take the Gospel out of Asia into Europe. He crossed the Hellespont into Macedonia and made his way to the city of Philippi, the principal city in that area. In Philippi, the message of the risen Savior found its way into the hearts of some with whom Paul and his company met by the river for prayer. Luke, the writer of the Gospel that bears his name, tells the story in Acts:

> And it came to pass, as we went to prayer, a certain damsel possessed with a spirit of divination met us, which brought her masters much gain by soothsaying: The same followed Paul and us, and cried, saying, These men are the servants of the most high God, which show unto us the way of salvation. And this did she many days. But Paul, being grieved, turned and said to the spirit, I command thee in the name of Jesus Christ to come out of her. And he came out the same hour.[162]

The demon that inhabited this girl in Philippi manifested its presence by allowing the girl to predict future events, evidently with some degree of accuracy. She was a slave, whose masters would charge money for others to come into her presence so that she could predict future events in their lives. An analysis of her statements concerning the Apostle Paul and his team will not be surprising in light of previously examined Scriptures. She asserted, "These men are the servants of the most high God, which show unto us the way of salvation." There was nothing wrong with what she was saying at all. Paul, Luke, Timothy, Silas, and whoever else may have been in the missionary team were indeed servants of God and their primary purpose was, in fact, to show the Philippians the way of salvation. The Apostle to the Gentiles, however, was anything but excited by this girl's testimony concerning him. He put up with it for many days, but eventually said to the spirit, "I command thee in the name of Jesus Christ to come out of her." This story seems consistent with the stories of demon-possessed people in the Gospels. The demon always spoke the truth, the man of God (or Son of God) was grieved to the point of forbidding the demon to speak, and the demon was cast out.

How does all of this pertain to music in a local church? Admittedly, music never comes into the narratives that relate these accounts. How is it that a principle of music can be drawn from passages that do not even mention music? The principle to be drawn is one that is much broader than just music, but it certainly includes the discussion of music. The essential truth illustrated by the demons, their speech, and their being cast out is this: God is not only interested that the truth go forth, but He is also concerned that the vehicle that bears the truth be pure. Jesus did not rejoice in the witness of demons, even though their witness was completely true. Paul did not rejoice that a demon-possessed diviner attested to his purpose of mission, even though what she said was accurate. It is not acceptable to God to have the truth go forth by just any means. The means by which the truth goes forth must be approved by Him and must be deemed by Him to be pure.

To present an argument from consistency, consider the following two examples of the truth being borne by an impure vehicle. Suppose I were to begin to announce in my ministry that I was embarking on a Christian alcohol ministry. From this time on, I would no longer focus my attention on preaching, but on selling beer, wine, whiskey, and other forms of alcoholic beverage. There would be many who would denounce such a ministry as illegitimate. They would say that the Word of God strongly denounces alcohol and pronounces those who use it to be foolish.[163] I might respond, "But you don't understand. Every one of my whiskey bottles will contain the plan of salvation on the label. I will only buy my materials from Christian farmers." Those opposed would rightly respond that when a man wants to get drunk, he pays little or no attention to the message on the label. Indeed, there are those who couldn't care less if the bottle says Seagram's or Scope; they drink either one for its alcohol content. Anyone who would argue against my Christian alcohol ministry would be right to do so. The problem is not that I am trying to get the Gospel out; the problem is that the vehicle that I chose is impure and thus negates the effect of the Gospel.

Similarly, suppose I began to announce that I was to embark on a ministry of Christian prostitution. All of the women who work in my ministry will be born-again Christians, leaving a Gospel tract with every client before they part company. The very idea should disgust God's people. The problem, once again, is not that the Gospel would go forth, but that the vehicle of carrying the Gospel would be impure.

In either the alcohol or the prostitution "ministry" there is obvious discrepancy between the truth and the vehicle chosen to present it. The inconsistency causes us to either be amused or to reel in horror, and rightly so. Consistency demands the same horror when we think of a demon proclaiming the deity of Christ or the legitimacy of Paul's apostolic ministry. Consistency also demands horror when we think of using sensual, Satanic rock music to present a message of truth. The principle of the vehicle of truth being pure is most plainly stated by God Himself through His prophet Isaiah: "Depart ye, depart ye, go ye out from thence, touch no unclean thing; go ye out of the midst of her; *be ye clean, that bear the vessels of the LORD.*"[164]

There are many other Bible principles regarding music that are beyond the scope of this book. In the debate between traditional music and CCM, however, the argument is won or lost over the issue of morality in music. Can a Christian present an image of a holy God by presenting truth through a vehicle that the world calls Satanic and sensual? If there is immorality in music, then the Bible principle of the vehicle of the truth demands that we reject all immoral music, regardless of the crowds it may bring in, regardless of the popularity it may bring, and regardless of any other supposed benefit that might come as a result of using it.

CHAPTER 13:
BODY LANGUAGE

One of the issues confronting Western culture today is the issue of tattoos on both men and women. There was a day when body art was reserved for military men, many of whom decided to follow the crowd and get a tattoo when they were still in their late teens or early twenties. Many former sailors, marines, soldiers, and airmen regretted in later years what they had done to their bodies in early manhood. While society frowned upon the idea of a tattoo, there was really nothing that could be done about it because a tattoo was permanent. Modern technology has made it possible to remove unwanted tattoos, much to the relief of some who had long regretted yielding their skin to a body artist in the first place.

Society's view of tattoos has changed, however, if the number of tattoo parlors and people wearing tattoos is any indication. Stores that once were either vacant or dedicated to something else are now tattoo parlors. One seems to see more advertisement for body artists that ever before. To a child of God wanting to be in style in modern culture, the question of whether or not to get a tattoo might arise. Would it be wrong, for example, to get a cross tattooed to one's arm? What about the phrase "Jesus Saves"? While the Bible does not mention the word *tattoo*, there is an Old Testament reference to the practice of body art. This statement is not repeated in the New Testament, however. Therefore it may be possible that it falls into the same category as the Old Testament Jewish sacrifice: binding for the Jew, but not for the Christian because it was fulfilled in Christ.

Before looking at New Testament principles that affect this discussion, it will be necessary first to understand the practice of body art through the centuries. The practice was very clearly prohibited as far as the Old Testament Jews were concerned. God told His people, "Ye shall not make any cuttings in your flesh for the dead, nor print any marks upon you: I am the LORD."[165] The practice of mutilating the body was a prevalent practice among many cultures of antiquity, especially in relation to the dead. Whenever a person would die, the friends and relatives would begin to beat and cut themselves until the blood freely flowed. The practice was evidently not just reserved for funerals, but came to be a part of the worship of some idols. The prophets of Baal on Mount Carmel mutilated their bodies "after their manner" in trying to call down fire from heaven.[166] In fact, the practice was nearly universal among non-Jewish cultures, with only a few exceptions. As time progressed, there were more and more laws passed that prohibited the practice of mutilation for the dead.[167] Apparently, God saw mutilation for the dead and body printing in the same category, for He dealt with them in the same sentence of the law. It is interesting to note that whenever a culture begins to condone printed marks on the human body, it is not long before some type of mutilation follows. God prohibited both for His people.

There can be no doubt that God disallowed body printing for the Old Testament Jews, but there are many prohibitions that held true for the Jews that are not binding upon Christians today. For an example of such a prohibition, one need only look to the previous verse in the Book of Leviticus: "Ye shall not round the corners of your heads, neither shalt thou mar the corners of thy beard."[168] While the exact meanings of these two practices may be debated as they related to Israel, there is virtually no one today who insists that these regulations are binding upon Christians. Those who do see a Christian regulation in these verses fail to properly distinguish Israel and the Church, a distinction that, of necessity, must be assiduously maintained. Jewish culture included the maintenance of a beard for men while Western culture today commonly rejects the full beard, or at least sees it as somewhat of an anomaly. If Leviticus prohibits tattoos, however, then it also must prohibit the practice of shaving, for both prohibitions appear in the same context of the same passage.

At the same time, the law of God can give principles by which Christians can live because it reveals the mind of God. While these regulations were quite literal for the Jews and while they are no longer binding for Christians today, they are valuable in revealing the mind of God as it affects culture. God wanted a distinction between the appearance of Jews and the appearance of the surrounding cultures. He wanted there to be a difference that was easily recognizable. God still wants such a distinction today between Christians and the world. He told the Roman believers, "Be not conformed to this world."[169] There were certain elements of culture that were to be discarded after salvation because they contradicted God's will for man. Evidently, there are some aspects of culture that God cares nothing about. For instance, in North America, it is cultural to drive on the right side of the road. In Great Britain, it is cultural to drive on the left side of the road. There really is no right or wrong with either cultural norm, so long as everyone does the same thing. There are elements of culture, however, that have a basis in sinful practices. Believers must reject these elements of culture.

Gentile culture of the first century had its wicked elements, to be sure. The Apostle Paul told the Ephesian church,

> This I say therefore, and testify in the Lord, that ye henceforth walk not as other Gentiles walk, in the vanity of their mind, Having the understanding darkened, being alienated from the life of God through the ignorance that is in them, because of the blindness of their heart: Who being past feeling have given themselves over unto lasciviousness, to work all uncleanness with greediness. But ye have not so learned Christ.[170]

The Apostle Paul went on to remind the Ephesians of some things that he had previously taught them, namely, that Christianity must repudiate elements of culture that are contrary to the will of God. The word *lasciviousness* means "lack of self-constraint which involves one in conduct that violates all bounds of what is socially acceptable, self-abandonment."[171] Peter used this word to describe the lifestyle of Sodom in the days of Lot.[172] This kind of behavior resulted in sexual immorality, both heterosexual and homosexual. It also included the problem of greediness, a universal vice that seems to be growing more and more overt in modern times. As one looks around at modern Western culture today, he can see a pattern of more and more aspects of culturally acceptable practices that are in opposition to the Gospel of Christ. It is up to the Christian, then, to discern which aspects of culture are rooted in lasciviousness and which aspects of culture are innocuous.

Into which category, then, does the subject of body printing fall? Is it merely an innocuous absurdity of culture, or it is the result of something darker? Bible answers to these questions must rely heavily, if not exclusively, upon the New Testament because of the essential difference between Israel and the Church. If tattoos are wrong for believers, there will be New Testament principles that point the child of God to that conclusion.

There are at least three appropriate principles from the New Testament that deal with the subject of tattoos. The first is a very broad principle that affects many areas of life: "Abstain from all appearance of evil."[173] Christians are to never involve themselves in practices that might raise a question in anyone's mind as to whether or not they are involved in wrongdoing. For example, for a married man to enter a motel room with an unmarried woman, spend several hours with her in private, and then leave with her would cause people to wonder if the couple had been involved in adultery. Even if the two were talking business for the entire time they were together, such a meeting in such a place would be wrong for the child of God because it gives the appearance of evil. There are other ways to talk business between a man and a woman without giving unsaved people opportunity to assume that sin has taken place. This principle has far-reaching consequences when evaluating different aspects of culture.

In order to apply this principle to the subject of body printing and tattoos, it is necessary to research some non-Christian ideas about the subject of tattoos and body printing. Although it admits that there would be some who would disagree, this secular source asserts the following about tattoos:

> Today, people choose to be tattooed for cosmetic, sentimental/memorial, religious, and magical reasons, and to symbolize their belonging to or identification with particular groups, including criminal gangs… but also a particular ethnic group or law-abiding subculture. Some Māori still choose to wear intricate moko on their faces. In Laos, Cambodia, and Thailand, the yantra tattoo is used for protection against evil and increase [sic] luck.[174]

Although not every reason listed by this source is contrary to New Testament principles, there are some reasons that the source lists for tattoos that are definitely pagan. An example would be "magical reasons" for tattoos. When the Gospel took root in Ephesus, one of the results was the burning of books that formerly instructed believers in occult practices.[175] The Gospel and the occult are definitely at odds with each other. In fact, the Bible predicts a day when the central figure in the Gospel, Jesus Christ, will destroy utterly and finally the founder of the occult, Satan. Since there are some unsaved people who identify tattoos with the occult, could a Christian wear a tattoo and still avoid the appearance of evil? Does wearing a tattoo that might be misconstrued to be of the occult demonstrate a holy God to the onlookers in the world? The same questions apply to the tattoo's association with gangs and superstition (good luck and protection from evil). When the average American looks at a person wearing a tattoo, he most likely does not immediately assume that the wearer of the body art is a separated Christian. He may not necessarily think that the person sporting the marks is hell bound, but neither does he immediately think, "This man (or woman) must be a Christian." The point is, however, that there are definitely evil cultural associations with some tattoos, associations that the Christian is to avoid. The reason for the association of tattoos with unbelievers is not hard to find.

> Historically, a decline in traditional tribal tattooing in Europe occurred with the spread of Christianity. … A poll conducted online in July 2003 estimated that 16% of all adults in the United States have at least one tattoo. The highest incidence of tattoos was found among the gay, lesbian and bisexual population (31%) and among Americans ages 25 to 29 years (36%) and 30 to 39 years (28%).[176]

If nearly one third of gays, lesbians, and bisexuals have tattoos, then there could potentially be the mistake of identification with these lifestyles. Would the Christian trying to portray a holy God to the unsaved world want to have others mistake him for a gay, lesbian, or bisexual? Is that the best way to reflect the holiness of God? More can be said about the homosexual and bisexual lifestyles and the tattoos they wear, but that topic is saved for the discussion of another New Testament principle.

The secular world provides other reasons for the child of God not to wear tattoos because of their "appearance of evil."

> In the United States many prisoners and criminal gangs use distinctive tattoos to indicate facts about their criminal behavior, prison sentences, and organizational affiliation. ... Insofar as this cultural or subculture [sic] use of tattoos predates the widespread popularity of tattoos in the general population, tattoos are still associated with criminality. ... Tattoos can have additional negative associations for women; "tramp stamp/slag tag/slutter-fly" and other similarly derogatory slang phrases are sometimes used to describe a tattoo on a woman's lower back.[177]

It is hard to argue with the fact that these symbols give the appearance of evil, at least in the minds of some in the unsaved world. In order to avoid this appearance, the child of God would be wise to refuse all body art altogether, especially permanent markings.

While researching for this chapter, I met a pastor of a Baptist church in the Mountain states. As a young man, he had been in the U.S. Navy both prior and subsequent to his salvation. Before he was saved, he got a pair of tattoos, one on each arm. After he was saved, he took a Bible with him back to his destroyer and was ridiculed by every other member of the crew. No one else on board, not even the ship's chaplain, was saved, and this young Christian bowed to the pressure and went back to many of his worldly habits that he had practiced before salvation. One night he staggered into his rack, drunk. The next morning, he did not remember where he had been the night before, but he did notice a pain in his left arm. It was not long before he recognized the pain as the discomfort that accompanies a new tattoo.

As the years passed, this man grew in the Lord until one day God called him to be a pastor. In the course of his personal witnessing one day, he encountered a man with many spiritual questions. The pastor answered every one of them and then explained, "I know these answers because I am a pastor." The man was immediately taken aback. He instantly contradicted this pastor, saying that God would never call any man to be a pastor who would do something so awful as get a tattoo. While the man's theology was inaccurate, the truth of the appearance of evil is obvious from his encounter with the pastor. Because of this pastor's permanent tattoo and its accompanying appearance of evil, he refuses to ever wear a short-sleeved shirt in public. Even in front of his children, he wore long sleeves so that the appearance of evil would at least be covered.

To be sure, not all in the unsaved world today are as opposed to tattoos as was this one man who spoke with this pastor, but the truth is that tattoos, more or less, are often associated with some kind of evil. When a person wears a garment that partially obscures the tattoo, the observer has no way of knowing whether the tattoo is a wicked symbol or not. He is left to guess whether this tattoo is vile or not.

According to some, the negative connotations of tattoos are not as bad or as universal as they once were.[178] In fact, if this were the only Bible principle governing the idea of tattoos, then there might theoretically come a day when it would be permissible for a Christian to get a tattoo. The cultural appearance of evil in a tattoo would have to be totally erased, however, in order for this to occur. From its history, there seems to be no time when the tattoo was totally devoid of wicked implications and thus the appearance of evil. Since God says to abstain from all appearance of evil and since a tattoo can give the appearance of evil, can a Christian get a tattoo and still keep from falling off of God's cliff of the appearance of evil? Remember that appearance of evil is not simply one author's fence; it is a Bible cliff.

While the first principle of the New Testament relating to tattoos is the appearance of evil, the second principle is, perhaps, a little more complicated to define. The second principle relates to the fact that our bodies belong to God. The Apostle Paul was surprised that the Corinthian church either did not know this fact or had not kept it in the forefront of their minds. He exclaimed to them, "What! Know ye not that your body is the temple of the Holy Ghost which is in you, which ye have of God, and ye are not your own?"[179] The Spirit of God indwells the believer's body similarly to the way the glory of God dwelt in the tabernacle in the Old Testament. There were times when God's glory was quite visible in the Tabernacle of Moses' day and the Temple of Solomon's day. The significant difference between God's glory in the Tabernacle/Temple and God's indwelling of the believer is that God's glory came and went from the Jewish place of worship. The Spirit of God abides with the believer forever, according to the promise of

Jesus.[180] Just as the Tabernacle was important to God in the Old Testament, the body of a believer is important to God in the New Testament. After reminding them that they were the temple of God, Paul told the Corinthian church, "If any man defile the temple of God, him shall God destroy; for the temple of God is holy, which temple ye are."[181]

There is a delicate balance to maintain at this point. Without a doubt, there are those in the Western culture today who worship the human body. They do what they do so that they can have the best physique or the greatest quality of physical life. They worship those who have attained the kind of body that they seek and consume their time with making their bodies more and more into the fantastical image that they have in their minds. On the other end of the spectrum are those who, like the heathen of antiquity, mutilate and disfigure their bodies. Whether it is putting a bone through the nose, or piercing the body in countless places, the practice of physical disfiguring seems to indicate dissatisfaction with the human body.

The world today has a concept called "self-esteem" that generally refers to thinking good thoughts and feeling good about oneself. The concept of self-esteem has been taken to an extreme to where the secular world decries those who would preach that man is a sinner. The idea of self-esteem is close to a Bible truth, however. The Bible truth is self-acceptance: that you should not so much see yourself as inherently good, but see yourself as an example of God's goodness. It is vitally important that a person accept whom God has made him to be. David said it this way: "I will praise thee, for I am fearfully and wonderfully made."[182] David's praise was not directed toward himself ("I'm good"), but it was directed toward God who gave David everything that he had. David had a real sense of satisfaction in the person whom God had made him to be. He did not look at himself and wish that something were vastly different about him. He did not think that God had somehow made a mistake by making him the youngest, the ruddiest, or the fairest. He simply looked at his physical and mental characteristics as evidence of God's greatness and saw them as a reason to praise Him. When a person begins to permanently disfigure his body, he sends a message, intended or not, to all those around him. He says, "I am not pleased with myself as God has made me to be, and I want to make some permanent changes." For a child of God whose body is God's temple, this message amounts to an indictment against God Himself. There are some in the unsaved world who get this connection. In fact, some secular studies have connected body printing and tattoos with low self-esteem.[183] While the secular idea of self-esteem is not the same as the Bible idea of self-acceptance, the symptoms of a person who lacks self-acceptance and self-esteem are the same. Before a person makes permanent changes to his body, he must come to grips with the fact that permanent changes to his body may imply dissatisfaction with his body. For others to see him, know he is a Christian, and perceive that he is dissatisfied with who God has made him to be, would constitute a bad reflection upon God. Before the Christian gets a tattoo, he must answer some questions. Will I communicate a message of dissatisfaction with whom God has made me to be by getting this tattoo? Is it possible that my tattoo will send a message to those around me that I am discontent with God's working in my life?

The third principle that a Christian must consider before getting a tattoo is the principle of conformity. The Apostle Paul makes it very plain: "Be not conformed to this world."[184] The Greek word in this verse that is translated *conformed*, meaning "to form according to a pattern or mold, form/model after,"[185] has found its way into English by way of transliteration. Today, when an electrical appliance fails to work properly, the repairman will consult a schematic of the system. The schematic tells the person building the appliance and the one attempting to repair it where each component should go and what it should do. The schematic of a washing machine, for example, tells where the electricity flows, what motors it turns, what capacitors control the flow of current, what valves are opened and closed by the current, and so forth. The world has a schematic for humanity, just as the appliance company has a schematic for its washing machine. The god of this world sets the schematic and dictates how each aspect of human existence is to function. As god of this world, Satan not only sets the marching orders for the world's system, but he also has an ongoing war with God Himself. Satan can do nothing to hurt God in any way because God is all-powerful. Therefore, since he cannot hurt God, he strikes at God's heart by destroying God's most wonderful aspect of creation: man. Only man is made in the image of God and only man has the capacity for free choice. Satan realizes that God's love for man is so great that he can only strike out at God by striking out at man. Therefore, as he designs the schematic for the world's system, he makes certain that the system will be destructive to man.

Little wonder that Christians are not to live their lives in conformity to the world's schematic. To do so would be hurtful to God and self-destructive for man. The principle of conformity affects the discussion of tattoos in this way: if the motivation to get a tattoo is to be like the world, then getting a tattoo is morally suspect, at best.

At this point, it is important to insert an explanation regarding conformity to the world. Some common practices of life make sense to do just because of their own merits. For example, in the United States, it is popular to launder one's clothes after wearing them. In fact, by the standards of the rest of the world, American standards of washing clothes may be somewhat extravagant. I have met very few Americans who do not wash their clothes after wearing them once. This practice is not a wicked plot of Satan to strike out against God, even though almost everyone in the American "world" does it. (I had a roommate in college that constituted a notable exception to this American practice, much to the dismay and discomfort of all of the rest of us Americans in the room. I began to wonder at one point if he had ever washed his clothes the entire semester.) There is a difference between practices that are merely cultural and practices that are sinfully motivated. At the same time, there are cultural practices that are motivated by the influence of Christianity and practices that are motivated by a rebellion against Christian culture. It requires discernment and some extracurricular study to ascertain which elements are merely cultural and which elements are worldly.

Whenever a person's motivation is wrong, the actions that he performs will almost invariably be wrong. Accordingly, if a person wants to be like the world, whatever he does based upon that motivation will probably be wrong. With respect to tattoos, while the practice is more visibly prevalent today than it has ever been before, it is a gross exaggeration to say that everyone is getting a tattoo these days. Some psychologists have tied the practice to a more rebellious sector of society, although others dispute these findings.[186] Those getting a tattoo, for the most part, have other problems with sin, and the printed marks on their body only serve as outward marks of inward bondage to a wicked world system. If a Christian decides to get a tattoo, he must ask himself, "Why am I doing this? Is it just to be like other people that I know, or am I doing this to show to the world that I belong to God and want to be more like His Son Jesus Christ?"

The same three principles, the appearance of evil, self-acceptance, and nonconformity to the world, also affect the discussion of whether or not a person should get multiple body piercings. Body piercing is closer to self-mutilation than printed marks on the body. Many who oppose multiple body piercings run into a problem of consistency because of the age-old practice of piercing the ear. The question rightly surfaces, "If it is wrong to have a pierced eyebrow, why it is permissible to have a pierced ear?"[187] In order to answer this question, it will be necessary to look at the three Bible principles applying to tattoos and apply them to the subject of piercing the body.

The first principle is the principle of the appearance of evil. As stated before, God does not want His child to raise a question in the mind of another person as to whether or not he is involved in evil. The essential question, then, is this: Do people view the practice of piercing the ear as identification with evil? While there was a time in the United States when the majority of women did not pierce their ears, the practice has been common worldwide since ancient times. In the Old Testament, both men and women are recorded to have pierced their ears, although the practice is not actually condoned, with one exception.[188] As has been already noted, Israel was forbidden to make "cuttings in your flesh for the dead,"[189] but the practice of boring through the ear as a sign of voluntary servitude was actually commanded in the Old Testament law (this is the one exception).[190] It would seem that God did not have a problem with a person boring a hole in his ear. Accordingly, today, when a woman pierces her ear with the intent of wearing ornamental earrings, there is probably no prevalent association with evil that observers make in their minds.

The opposite can often be true when the earring appears in a man's ear, however. Earrings in men have been used as a symbol of homosexuality, as well as effeminate and bisexual behavior.[191] Although this association is not necessarily consistent in its use, there are definitely sectors of culture that would associate male earrings with the sodomite lifestyle. Other lifestyles that popularized male earrings were popular musicians, punk rock musicians, and hippies. All of these carried definite elements of culture that were decidedly anti-Christian. The Christian man who wants to get an earring must answer some questions before making the decision. Might some people view my earring as an identification with ungodly aspects of culture? Will this earring unmistakably show others that the God I serve is holy? While there is evidently no appearance of evil for a woman to wear an earring, there is the possibility of the appearance of evil for a man to do so.

The practice of body piercing is tied to the homosexual lifestyle, being made popular by homosexuals who claim to derive gratification from inflicted pain upon a human body, either their own or someone else's.[192] Body piercing has its roots in this lifestyle and behavior. According to the Apostle Paul, homosexual behavior is the result of man's rebellion against God.

> Because that, when they knew God, they glorified him not as God, neither were thankful; ... Who changed the truth of God into a lie, and worshipped and served the creature more than the Creator, who is blessed for ever. Amen. For this cause God gave them up unto vile affections: for even their women did change the natural use into that which is against nature: And likewise also the men, leaving the natural use of the woman, burned in their lust one toward another; men with men working that which is unseemly, and receiving in themselves that recompence of their error which was meet. And even as they did not like to retain God in their knowledge, God gave them over to a reprobate mind, to do those things which are not convenient.[193]

Paul later told Timothy that homosexuality, along with many other sins, is contrary to the doctrine of the Gospel.[194] Given that the practice of body piercing has its roots in homosexuality and given that God wants His people to abstain from the appearance of evil, would it be worth the risk of identifying with a lifestyle that God condemns just to get some part of the body pierced?

The very roots of body piercing directly contradict the principle of taking care of the body because it is the temple of God. There seems to be dissatisfaction within the homosexual community for God's design in life. A man dislikes the fact that he is male and so decides to become transgender or bisexual. His chosen sexual orientation is "that which is against nature" and "unseemly"[195] in the sight of God. Indeed, his behavior is evidence of his desire to expunge God from every aspect of his life.[196] By contrast, the child of God realizes that his body is the result of God's wonderful design that should evoke praise to Him, rather than dissatisfaction. Since body piercing publicly displays dissatisfaction with God's design, it violates the principle of the Christian's body being the temple of God. As a child of God, would piercing my body best demonstrate to the world that I am doing everything I can to take care of my body because it is His temple?

The final principle of conformity to the world that was used to argue against tattoos comes into play with body piercing as well. Body piercing started as a practice of ungodly men in an effort to voice their opposition to God and His design for their lives. While there very well may be people who are not part of this original lifestyle who participate in body piercing today, anyone who knows its roots could easily describe body piercing as the schematic of the world, a schematic that the Christian is commanded to avoid. If I as a believer pierce my body, am I doing it to be more Christ-like or am I doing it to be more like the world?

In short, when it comes to the subject of either permanent printed body art, or body piercing, there are three New Testament principles that directly affect the decision in a believer's life: first, the principle of abstaining from all appearance of evil; second, the principle of treating the body with care because it is the temple of God; and third, the principle of not being conformed to the world. Body art and body piercing have the definite appearance of evil in the eyes of many, and these practices give the appearance of dissatisfaction with God's design of the human body. In addition, they stem from a worldly, ungodly subculture. Can the believer, then, make these permanent changes to his body and accurately reflect the holiness of the God he serves?

CHAPTER 14:
TINSELTOWN

Hollywood. The very name brings certain images and lifestyles to a person's mind, even if he has not grown up in the United States of America. In fact, to many in the world, the lifestyle portrayed in motion pictures in the United States is synonymous with American culture. Many aspects of life today are directly affected by the content of American motion pictures or movies. Avid students of written history are fewer these days, but the numbers of people who can remember the movie about a particular figure are large indeed. Sociology is a topic that rarely tops best-selling book lists, but let a movie touch on an aspect of sociology and suddenly the world is filled with experts. Religion, politics, crime and punishment, racial issues, technology, science—all of these topics find their way into the production studio, onto the screen, and eventually into the homes of Americans.

For the child of God, the movie industry was once almost completely taboo. There were preachers by the droves who stood up and preached against the movie industry in general and "going to the movies" (attending the theater) in particular. There was a day when not attending movies was just another of the things that Christians didn't do. American Christians seem to have discovered the theater, however, in recent years with the result that there are fewer and fewer today who associate going to the movies with wickedness. Today, there are churches with fewer members than they might otherwise have because they have in their constitution a statement against going to movies in the theater. The church constitution is not the Bible, however. That is, doing something that one church forbids is not necessarily wrong just because the church forbids it. If the Bible forbids the practice, then it is wrong, regardless of what any church says. If the Bible does not forbid the practice, then there is certainly the possibility that a believer can engage in it and still be right with God.

The motion picture is another form of art that the believer will not find mentioned by name in the Word of God. There was no such thing as a movie, a movie theater, or a DVD when the Apostle Paul wrote under inspiration of the Spirit. However, there are some principles that guide the choices of a believer's life when it comes to his entertainment. These principles will be broader than just the issue of a person's choice in movies, but they will apply to movies.

The question of whether or not to attend the movie theater is one that has become more debated in recent years. Were the old-fashioned preachers right to preach against going to the movie theater, and what was their Bible basis for preaching against it? In order to answer these questions, it is first of all important to understand some concepts associated with the theater. When I was a teenager in the late 1990s, there was no doubt in the minds of unsaved teens as to why Christians did not attend the movies. The reason had nothing to do with the content of the films themselves. Whenever a teen couple went to see a movie, they were not primarily going to see the film. They went to capitalize on the two hours of darkness that accompanied seeing the movie. They could do a lot of things under cover of the theater's darkness that they would struggle to be able to get away with otherwise. When a teenager would get saved out of that culture and then be told in church that Christians do not go to the movies, he never even questioned why. He understood perfectly why the saved lifestyle was incompatible with what he used to do at the theater.

This association brings up a Bible principle with respect to the theater. Paul told the Thessalonian believers, "Abstain from all appearance of evil."[197] If a Christian wants to attend a movie theater, he must answer this question: Is it possible that my attendance at this theater might be construed by others as a chance to participate in something evil? To be sure, the sensual association with the movie theater is not a universal one, but the fact that it exists at all should make the theater at least suspect for the child of God.

In addition to the appearance of evil, there is another problem with the theater. Many theaters have posters lining their walls, each poster advertising either a film now playing or a film coming soon. Many of these posters are put together with the intent of causing the viewer to lust after an actor or actress, in direct violation of the Word of God. Paul told the Corinthians, "Flee fornication."[198] To stand there in the theater and view some of the posters advertising movies is not fleeing, but feeding fornication. Remember that sexual sin is always a sin of the mind before it ever becomes a sin of the body.[199] While a man or woman does not have to go to a movie theater to see pictures that feed fornication, the walls of the theater seem to exist for the purpose of feeding the wicked lust of man. The Apostle Paul's admonition to Timothy stands against the idea when he says, "Flee also youthful lusts."[200] Can the child of God really flee youthful lusts by placing himself in a location designed to feed them?

The greatest problem with the theater, however, is not the appearance of evil, or even the lust that is so essential to the entire movie industry. The greatest problem is the content of the films themselves. God's preachers have been preaching against Hollywood for years because Hollywood has created a mindset that is opposed to God and His Word.

In the Southeast, where I have been brought up all my life and where I now call home, there was a day when the people, as a rule, were quite poor. Friends of mine, who are old enough to be called my adopted parents, tell me that families tended to be large, while houses tended to be very small, especially by modern standards. The bunk bed was considered one of the greatest inventions in the history of man because there was only one room for as many as eight or more children. Mama and Daddy had a bedroom for themselves, and the children had a bedroom to share. Those who grew up in the Southeast during that time have told me, "Paul, when we were growing up, we didn't have anything. All of us were happy, though, because we didn't know anybody who had anything." No one told them that every child had to have his own separate bedroom. No one had communicated to them that toys were necessary to happiness. No one had ever elucidated to them the dire necessity of an extensive wardrobe for each child. They just did not know that these material things of life were essential to happiness.

Gradually, however, that ignorance changed. Photographs came to be strung together in a line so that there were now two types of photography: still photography and motion photography. In motion photography, the pictures actually moved to create a form of realism never before experienced. The moving pictures came to be called "movies," and before long, the money spent on movies developed motion pictures into one of the largest sectors of the entertainment industry. America, and indeed, all of Western Europe had gone to the movies. The movies that they went to see showed them images of people living in more lavish conditions. These conditions were being portrayed as completely normal to the place where people began to feel unusual if they didn't measure up to this artificial standard portrayed in the movies. Reality itself began to change.

Despite the introduction of the television into American life, the movie theater has retained its popularity as a means of American entertainment, netting billions of dollars of profits every year. To some, the lives of the actors and actresses have become as newsworthy as the movements of armies on the world scene. Even directors and producers have achieved some degree of fame, simply because of their connection to the movie industry.

Movies have proven to have the power to influence the thinking of their patrons, and because of their popularity, of society as a whole. The humble material surroundings of a past generation have given way to more lavish dwellings, simply because people believe they need more and nicer things. The ideas of interaction with the opposite gender have changed, too, as a result of a drastic change in thinking traceable to movies. Some have even denounced the Hollywood thinking about romance as the root of so many marital problems in modern society.[201]

The Bible, while not ever mentioning movies, does deal with the dynamic involved in the movies. Movies communicate with the viewer in two ways: sight and sound. There is one notable example of a man in the Bible whose thinking was drastically changed by sight and sound.

His story starts off with great promise as he rubs shoulders with one of the greatest servants of God of all time. Called the Friend of God,[202] Abram (his name was later changed to Abraham) established an early pattern of worshiping and serving the God of heaven. In his early years in Canaan, he traveled in the company of his nephew Lot, who, like Abram, was a wealthy man. The day came when Lot's servants and Abram's servants began to quarrel. Conceivably, there would have been disputes over water, grazing ground, mountain passages, and so forth as both men's servants vied for the best conditions for their respective flocks and herds. Specifically, the Bible says that "the land was not able to bear them, that they might dwell together: for their substance was great, so that they could not dwell together."[203] Because of the fighting that was taking place between the servants of the two men, Abram decided to allow Lot to choose another place for his abode. He implored Lot:

Let there be no strife, I pray thee, between me and thee, and between my herdmen and thy herdmen; for we be brethren. Is not the whole land before thee? Separate thyself, I pray thee, from me: if thou wilt take the left hand, then I will go to the right; or if thou depart to the right hand, then I will go to the left.[204]

Abram was taking the high road by giving his nephew the choice. It was a choice, however, that Lot was ill equipped to make because of the spiritual ramifications. God reveals the motivation of Lot's heart in making his decisions:

And Lot lifted up his eyes, and beheld all the plain of Jordan, that it was well watered every where, before the LORD destroyed Sodom and Gomorrah, even as the garden of the LORD, like the land of Egypt, as thou comest unto Zoar. Then Lot chose him all the plain of Jordan; and Lot journeyed east: and they separated themselves the one from the other. Abram dwelled in the land of Canaan, and Lot dwelled in the cities of the plain, and pitched his tent toward Sodom. But the men of Sodom were wicked and sinners before the LORD exceedingly.[205]

This is the first significant mention of Lot in the Scripture, but it is only the beginning of what would become one of Scripture's greatest tragedies.

It was not long after pitching his tent toward Sodom that Lot decided to move into the city of Sodom. While Scripture says nothing of the details of this move, there can be no doubt that it occurred. Indeed, the next chapter in the story of Lot's life finds him living in Sodom.[206] He, along with the rest of the cities of the plain, was taken captive by a foreign confederacy of kings and, in turn, liberated by Abram's armed servants. While Lot is not a main character in the events of the story, which includes the colorful and controversial character Melchizedek, it is interesting to note that he did not stay outside the city of Sodom, deciding rather to move within its boundaries.

The next mention of Lot as a character comes in the twilight of Sodom's existence as a city. Having been disgusted long enough with Sodom's perversion, God and two angels had come down to reveal to Abraham (his name had been changed by this time) His plan to destroy the city. The two angels evidently continued on into Sodom. Not long after coming into the city, they met Lot himself: "And there came two angels to Sodom at even; and Lot sat in the gate of Sodom: and Lot seeing them rose up to meet them; and he bowed himself with his face toward the ground."[207] Evidently, the fact that Lot was sitting at the gate of the city was an evidence of his holding some kind of political or judicial office. Later on, the men of Sodom would say of Lot, "He will needs be a judge,"[208] indicating that his position at the gate was some kind of an official position. Whatever happened in Lot's life, he evidently came to the place where he was comfortable in the wicked city of Sodom. In relating the initial choice that Lot made, the Scripture inserts, "But the men of Sodom were wicked and sinners before the LORD exceedingly."[209] Somehow, Lot got to the place where their wickedness did not bother him, at least not enough to keep him from the comforts and protection of living in the city. The fact that he gained some kind of position in the gate of the city also indicates that he may have achieved a measure of popularity there in Sodom. At any rate, there is a progression in his life from pitching his tent toward Sodom, to living in Sodom, to sitting at the gate of Sodom. From the Genesis account, it seems that there might have come a change in Lot's spiritual thinking over time.

Further evidence of this change of thinking comes within the details of the story itself. In fact, the last chapter of Lot's life in the Biblical narrative presents some of the most grotesque sins known to man. Although the angels originally planned to spend the night in the streets of Sodom, so as to not be a burden on anyone, Lot eventually persuaded them not to attempt such a thing, but to join him at his house. Before long, however, Sodom's citizens showed their reason for God's displeasure.

> But before they lay down, the men of the city, even the men of Sodom, compassed the house round, both old and young, all the people from every quarter: And they called unto Lot, and said unto him, Where are the men which came in to thee this night? Bring them out unto us, that we may know them.[210]

The men of Sodom wanted to rape these heavenly visitors who had taken shelter in Lot's house. The phrase "that we may know them" refers to sexual relations, often relations that God condemned.[211] There was apparently not a man in the entire city who was not in this lustful mob intent on wickedness. Anyone right with God would want to rebuke the mob and denounce such wickedness and perversion. Lot's response to them was quite disappointing, however. In fact, it revealed depravity in his own heart, depravity that he had evidently learned in his new home of Sodom.

Lot went out of his house to address the crowd:

> I pray you, brethren, do not so wickedly. Behold now, I have two daughters which have not known man; let me, I pray you, bring them out unto you, and do ye to them as is good in your eyes: only unto these men do nothing; for therefore came they under the shadow of my roof.[212]

It is at this point in the story that the depths of Lot's wicked thinking are exposed to the world. As the father of two daughters, I cannot conceive of anyone who would stoop so low as to offer his two virgin daughters to men of such twisted minds and perverted morals. Yet Lot, in an effort to placate the wicked crowd, was willing to sacrifice the purity of his daughters. Such a reprehensible action causes the reader to shrink in horror and ask himself the question, "How could anyone do such a thing?" Indeed, the answer to this question is of the utmost importance.

Lot did what he did because he thought the way he thought, or in the words of Solomon, "As he thinketh in his heart, so is he."[213] At one time, Lot had been under one of the greatest influences for good that the world has ever known. The name Abraham became so associated with a walk with God that he came to be called such things as "faithful Abraham"[214] and "the friend of God."[215] Lot had this influence early in life, but after the break with Abraham, he went further and further away from the influence of his godly uncle. The question of why Lot would do this is important because there is the possibility that people today could have their thinking changed just as Lot had his thinking changed. While no one today has the luxury of being with Abraham, we have something far better: the Word of God. There could be no greater influence than the pages of Scripture, yet it is conceivably possible to allow one's thinking to be changed to the point where a man begins to justify wickedness just as Lot did. It is also logical to conclude that whatever caused Lot to change his thinking, and consequently, his morals, could very well cause a believer today to change his thinking and morals.

So the question of Lot's story comes back again, How could Lot do such a thing as to offer his virgin daughters to perverts? The answer is not to be found in the Old Testament narrative. In fact, it would be difficult to prove unequivocally that Lot was saved if there were no New Testament commentary on his life. The New Testament commentary on Lot, however, allows the Bible student to see beyond the events of Lot's life to the motivations behind those events. It allows the story of Lot to span the centuries of time until it finds practical relevance today.

It was Peter, writing in his Second Epistle, who gave us the answers to the haunting questions about the story of Lot. Peter's reasoning includes far more than just Lot, but it does give insight into the story that is invaluable for answering the question of how Lot could do what he did. Peter's reasoning could be summarized as follows:

If God did not spare:
- The angels that rebelled with Lucifer
- The Antediluvian civilization
- Sodom and Gomorrah

But did deliver Lot, then He knows how to deliver His people and judge sinners.[216]

It is in the context of this broader argument that Peter gives the details about Lot. Specifically, Peter says that in judging Sodom and Gomorrah, God "delivered just Lot, vexed with the filthy conversation of the wicked."[217] This statement is the only statement in the Bible that indicates that Lot was ever a saved man. Lot was a "just" man, one who has been declared righteous before God. This bit of information is not exactly comforting because if Lot could do what he did as a saved man, then saved people today are likewise capable of despicable acts of depravity.

As a saved man, Lot was "vexed with the filthy conversation of the wicked." The word translated *vexed* means "to cause distress through oppressive means, subdue, torment, wear out, oppress."[218] As Lot went about his daily business in the city of Sodom, he found himself confronted with behavior that he knew to be sinful. Immorality was rife, and Lot knew it. The longer he stayed in the city, the more the wickedness of the city wore him down. It tormented him during his waking moments and haunted him at night before he went to sleep until he eventually got to the place where he found himself subdued and worn out. Eventually, fighting got to be too much and giving in to the sin around him was the easier route to take. Still, exactly how did Lot get to the place where he could offer his two daughters to Sodom? Peter again gives the answer.

In order to further explain his thoughts about Lot, Peter continues, "For that righteous man dwelling among them, in seeing and hearing, vexed his righteous soul from day to day with their unlawful deeds."[219] Finally, Peter gives the *modus operandi* of Lot's desensitizing process: seeing and hearing. It was in seeing and hearing that he tormented his soul, day in and day out. It was in seeing and hearing that his thinking was gradually changed. It was in seeing and hearing that his morals moved. It was in seeing and hearing that he decided to change his residence from the tent to the gate. It was in seeing and hearing that Lot changed his thinking to the place where he could offer his two virgin daughters to froward men.

Satan has not changed his tactics over the years. The Romans came to power after Sodom and Gomorrah were long gone, but they still offered the allurements of entertainment, where in the Coliseum, one could still see and hear all kinds of violence and wickedness. Rome passed off the scene, and the acting theater became the new means whereby sinful man could see and hear ungodly deeds. Men of God preached against the acting theater in days gone by because of its exposure of the people to wickedness through seeing and hearing. Today, technology has multiplied the effects of seeing and hearing by placing the potential to see and hear wickedness in almost every home in America. The movie has replaced the acting theater, and now the patron has the choice of seeing and hearing wickedness in the public movie theater or simply waiting until he is in the privacy of his home. Experience has shown that, like the saved man Lot, many Christians in good churches today have vexed their own souls by seeing and hearing the wickedness of the world through the movie industry.

When I was a teenager, there was a truism that circulated among us in the Christian school and church that I attended. We would say, "There is no way that I would ever go to the theater and watch that movie. I'll just wait until it comes out on video to watch it." We laughed at that saying, usually nervously, because while we could see the obvious inconsistency of it, we also knew that it was true too many times. For years, many

Christians have taken a strong stand against going to the movie theater because of the appearance of evil, but they have patronized the video store. There is a certain anonymity to the video store. While anyone with a cursory knowledge of the theater's schedule can tell what a person has watched at the theater, the plastic bag from the video store can hide the contents from the outside world so that no human being will ever know exactly what is in the bag. Now Internet companies like Netflix make the movie industry even more accessible and secret without the patron having to leave the privacy of his home. Christians have brought into their homes what they would have never watched in the theater. The same wickedness that was there in the theater is in their homes, however, with the same deleterious effects. Like Lot, Christians have tormented themselves by insisting that they see and hear the ungodly deeds of the world.

By contrast, the Apostle Paul told the Ephesians, "But fornication, and all uncleanness, or covetousness, let it not be once named among you, as becometh saints; Neither filthiness, nor foolish talking, nor jesting, which are not convenient."[220] Later on, Paul adds, "And have no fellowship with the unfruitful works of darkness, but rather reprove them. For it is a shame even to speak of those things which are done of them in secret."[221] Many of the movies of today take the very shameful things that Paul named and favorably display them before the minds of those seeing and hearing. So, like Lot, Christians find their morals moving to the place where they now see as innocuous what they once condemned.

As an evangelist, I am privileged to preach in Christian schools from time to time. While my ministry has not spanned the years that other ministries have, I have seen some changes among the Christian school students to whom I preach. There has come an increasing propensity to hear them take the name of God in vain like never before. This tendency is very disconcerting because of the holy character of God's name and His expressed opinions against using it as a swear word. I, along with many others, have asked the question, "Why do so many young people use God's name in vain today?" I think that the answer comes back to Peter's explanation of Lot. Young people today see and hear others take the name of God in vain until they come to view swearing as normal behavior. They no longer think anything of it because they have seen and heard much worse things than what they say and do. Even Lot still had a standard of morality. He viewed what the men of Sodom were doing as wicked, yet he failed to see how perverted his offered alternative was. So it is with Christians today. They have seen and heard so much wickedness, mostly by way of movies and television, that they recognize the existence of right and wrong but fail to see their own actions as wrong. The universal tendency of man is to view morality by comparison. The unsaved man views sin in relative terms, and we rightfully point out that right and wrong is an absolute standard set by God Himself. Unfortunately, many who profess to be believers also accept a relative standard of right and wrong, excusing themselves because they are not nearly as bad as much of what they have seen and heard.

The problem is that what we have seen and heard has affected our thinking. Recall that the devil has a schematic that he actively presents to man. If man runs his thinking according to this schematic, he will destroy himself and hurt his Creator. God commands believers to reject this schematic and renew their minds according to God's way of thinking as revealed in His Word. Is it possible to renew my mind according to God's Word while spending two hours a week mindlessly succumbing to the schematic of the world through what I see and hear?

Often, when a Christian decides to take steps to reflect the holiness of God in his entertainment habits, he will use technology that is available today to take out swearing and offensive language from television and movies. This kind of technological device has been seen as a panacea for the problem of godless entertainment, but there are definite drawbacks. For one, while it is possible to edit specific words from a script, it is impossible to edit a philosophy. A character who swears on screen does so because he has a wrong philosophy about life in general and God in particular. There is no device that prevents a person from seeing and hearing this wicked philosophy. The only way to prevent seeing and hearing it is to avoid the movie completely.

It is amazing to see the lengths to which Christians will go in order to keep their entertainment. I have seen God's people suffer through a scene of a movie in which God's name was taken in vain, immorality was encouraged, filthiness was exalted, and jesting was predominant, all in hopes that the movie would get better. It is as if we must watch some movie, even if it contains some things that are revolting to our God. While we don't like them, we put up with them, because, after all, we've got to watch something. In truth, I have never heard any of God's people say those exact words, but their behavior surely seems to communicate just such a truth.

Would to God we would sacrifice for God's work in the same way! Would to God we would say, "I know that this is hard and that it inconveniences me, but I must go witnessing for Christ to get the Gospel out."

While I was in lower Alabama for a revival meeting, a pastor friend of mine took me fishing and told me some stories of angling in the area. With the Mobile Bay and the Gulf of Mexico so close, many anglers in that part of the country prefer saltwater fishing to freshwater. I grew up freshwater fishing for bass and panfish and still enjoy pursuing them today. My friend related a story to me of angling in the brackish water near where the Mobile River meets the Mobile Bay. He said that there are some good sized bass in the brackish water there, some of them as large as twelve pounds. In order to get to them, the fisherman must wade through the brackish water, fishing as he goes. Any angler willing to wade through the water to get to where the fish are is likely to be rewarded by large fish and long fights. There is a risk involved, however. The brackish water is not only home to largemouth bass; it is also home to alligators. It is entirely conceivable for a man to be wading in the brackish water and have his leg become lunch for a lurking reptile. For some, this risk is negligible compared to the fishing rewards that the brackish water offers. Others, however, would be content to catch smaller fish and have the assurance of their limbs being intact at the end of the day.

In nearly every worthwhile activity of life, there is a risk involved. Some of life's greatest rewards reside next to some of life's greatest risks. The decision to forego or proceed should be based upon the answer to this question: Are the rewards to be gained greater than the risks to be taken? When it comes to entertainment, the child of God must ascertain the rewards of the entertainment and compare them with the spiritual risks of being desensitized through seeing and hearing. If it is possible to be entertained without the risk of seeing and hearing wickedness, then it would seem logical to choose a less dangerous form of entertainment. If there are twelve-pound bass in a pond with mown banks, why wade with the gators?

As one who studies the Bible as a part of my life's occupation, I have endeavored to find the idea of entertainment in the Scripture. There are mentions of entertainment, to be sure, but none of them have a positive light. For instance, in the Book of Exodus, while Moses was receiving the Ten Commandments from God, the people began to worship idols. In their worship, they "rose up to play."[222] This could hardly be a positive mention of the idea of entertainment, however. In fact, what Israel did that day brought the judgment of God upon the entire nation. Likewise, there is entertainment at the cross of Calvary as Roman soldiers gamble for the unique robe of Jesus Christ,[223] but this could hardly be classified as a positive mention.

There is the concept of rest in Scripture, in both Old and New Testaments, but this should not be confused with the concept of entertainment. God ordained one day out of seven, one year out of seven, and one year out of fifty, for Israel to rest. In the New Testament, Jesus told His disciples, "Come ye yourselves apart into a desert place, and rest a while,"[224] but this did not involve seeing and hearing wicked men in their wickedness. There may have been times to celebrate God's goodness, but the modern idea of entertainment seems to be foreign to the Scripture. If it is in God's Word, it certainly has a negative connotation every time it appears. It seems contrary to the will of God, then, to make such sacrifices for the sake of entertainment, especially when Satan's tool of wearing the believer down is in seeing and hearing.

Is it wrong for a Christian to attend the movie theater? The answer depends upon some answers to other questions. Can the Christian attending the movie guarantee that his attendance will not constitute the appearance of evil? Every bit as dangerous as attending the theater, however, is for the Christian to watch the movie in the privacy of his home and to allow the world to influence his thinking and vex his soul through seeing and hearing. Can the child of God who loves his holy Lord consistently tolerate man's affronts to His holiness? Can he honestly say that he loves God and voluntarily view men and women who are offending His character and breaking His heart? Any child of God concerned about holiness will find himself moving further and further away from any opportunity to see and hear wickedness on the screen.

CONCLUSION

There is a two-fold tragedy whenever a person refuses to recognize the importance of cliffs and fences. Stated another way, there are at least two casualties every time a child of God falls off a cliff. Obviously, the child of God who sins is a casualty, but God is affected as well. To call God a casualty is, perhaps, a stretch, but God's heart is broken and His holiness violated whenever His child falls off a cliff. God longs to be lifted up before wicked men, and when His child falls off the cliff into sin, His name is blasphemed among men. The heart of God for His people and for holiness demands that there be some fences built along the way to keep the edge of the cliff out of reach.

The other casualty is the offender himself. The omnipotent God is able to raise up other men who will accurately portray His holiness to the world around, but the man who sins is always hurt by his sin, sometimes irrevocably. A look at the spiritual disasters that have taken place in the absence of fences can be sobering, to say the least. The scars, the tears, the shattered lives and testimonies—all combine their voices in chorus to convince Christians of the importance of building fences in life.

There is a cliff near where I grew up, the bottom of which contains several wrecked automobiles from years gone by. To examine these debacles is sobering and causes the observer to wonder about the story that each one represents. The spiritual cliff is the same way. There, the wrecks of individual lives give observers pause as they contemplate the individual stories represented. The damage is not physical—twisted steel and broken glass. Rather it is the carnage of broken lives and shattered testimonies, tragedies that could have been avoided had there been a fence to protect the person from the cliff. Too often, the carnage is worst among the spiritually immature, either because no one told them the importance of building fences or because they rebelled against the fences that were already in place. Satan uses many different methods to dissuade a man from building a fence. Some have found the principles of Romans 14 blatantly violated and have used these violations as reason to forsake the idea of building fences in their lives. Others have assumed that they were invincible—too mature to need such petty regulations to keep them from falling. Whatever the reason for refusing to build a fence, the result is always as inevitable as it is tragic. Part of the purpose of this book has been to help avert the tragedies that befall those, simply because they do not build fences in their lives.

One such tragic story that comes to mind concerns a young man who was a friend of mine as we were in high school. Finding it easy to make friends quickly at the small Christian school that we attended, he was one of the most likable people that I have ever met. When he came to the school, he knew very little about the sports that our school made available (basketball, mainly, because you only need five people for a team), but we took him under our wing and taught him what we knew and what we were learning. Before long, he knew how to box out on the low post and get the rebound even from larger, taller opponents. He also developed a reputation for being a scrappy player on the court, playing with all his heart. He might dive out of bounds to save a loose ball or take a charge and be smashed into the wall. His shooting was not the best, but he was improving, and he was one of us—we were not all that great ourselves.

Basketball was our life during the winter days of school, but we did basketball a bit differently even than most Christian schools did it. Part of our daily regimen of practice included giving devotions to the team before we hit the court every day. My friend, in his proper turn, was expected to dig into the Bible for himself and come up with a principle from the Word of God to share with the rest of his team. Like all the rest of us, he did it, and did it fairly well. Every game day, I, as captain of the team, would give devotions to the team in the locker room before the game. It was a tremendous time of spiritual development for many of us. One of my teammates came to me one day, and I was able to lead him to Christ in the hallway of our school.

We all hated to see the end of the basketball season, mainly because we got bored with all the extra time we had. Sports in the winter months had kept us busy and worn out, so that we had little time for mischief.

together as husband and wife. In the meantime, should things not work out for them as a couple, neither would have given their heart to someone that they would not actually marry.

When they were finally allowed to go on their first date, he was twenty and she was eighteen. Even then, they were not to be alone: both sets of parents accompanied them on their first date. Throughout the dating process this couple was not allowed to be alone together. They could have voted in Presidential elections, but they could not date alone unchaperoned.

In today's society, such rules for people of this age seem a bit extreme. Surely no one could be happy living by such restraints as these. Yet the two, though there were times when they struggled, were submissive to the fences placed in their lives. They were told that if God put the two of them together, they would be grateful after their wedding day for the standards by which they were living.

After she completed one year of college, he asked her officially to marry him. A year later, he graduated with his bachelor's degree from college and she with an associate's degree. The two were married within a month of graduation. The ceremony seemed especially sweet, as if crowned by the smile of God Himself. Here were two young people who had not cheapened any of the perquisites of marriage by indulging in them before the proper time. They had lived within fences built a long way from the cliff, but there is no regret in their minds today.

These two are indeed grateful that they lived their dating lives within such "confining" fences. Today, they do give gifts to each other, each gift being much sweeter because they waited. Today, every aspect of marriage, whether simply holding hands, giving cards or gifts, time alone talking, or any other of the other blessings of the marital relationship, is a joy to them. Today, they would tell you that their marriage is stronger and sweeter simply because of the standards by which they lived while they were dating. Today, there is no doubt in their minds that the good things of marriage only got better because they waited.

Even greater than their own happiness at having lived such a separated life is the fact that those who saw them and knew them to be Christians noticed God's holiness reflected in their conduct. People are seldom surprised when unsaved couples take great liberties with each other in premarital relationships. These two were God's children, however. As God's children, they endeavored to reflect His holiness in their lives. Their success in reflecting God's holiness brought with it the added blessings of happiness, purity, and safety—all because they lived by some fences in their lives. May we always be seeking to live a life of holiness as God has commanded, and may we at the same time remember to live for the edification of other believers. Holiness and harmony—the balance of these should characterize everything that is done with respect to cliffs and fences. Then let us build fences, seeing first the holiness of God, then the cliff itself and its slippery edge. Let us seek to pass on the fences honestly and fairly to those in our spheres of influence, so that neither we nor they end up in that awful tragedy, the tragedy of being shattered at the base of an avoidable cliff.

NOTES

Chapter One

[1] It will always be easy for men who look at the past to be judgmental. After all, hindsight is 20/20. The rightness or wrongness of these standards of the past is not the purpose of this chapter or this book.

[2] Numbers 16:36–40.

[3] *Theological Wordbook of the Old Testament,* by R. Laird Harris, et al. (Chicago: Moody Press, 1980). S.v. קָדַשׁ. Part of Bible Works, LLC © 2001, version 5. Hereafter, this work will be abbreviated *TWOT*.

[4] Exodus 29:21,37; 30:1–7, etc.

[5] *TWOT,* s.v. קֹדֶשׁ.

[6] Exodus 19:6.

[7] Exodus 20:8; Numbers 15:32–36.

[8] Malachi 2:11.

[9] Isaiah 6:1–3; Revelation 4:8.

[10] Isaiah 65:1.

[11] Acts 17:30.

[12] Ephesians 1:22–23.

[13] Acts 10:9–16.

[14] *Greek-English Lexicon of the New Testament and Other Early Christian Literature,* Third Ed. by W. F. Arnt, et al. (Chicago: The University of Chicago Press, 2000). Part of Bible Works, LLC © 2001, version 5. S.v. ἅγιος. Hereafter, this work will be abbreviated *BDAG.*

[15] *Ibid.* Abbreviations in the original have been spelled out for the sake of clarity.

[16] Habakkuk 1:12–13.

[17] Ephesians 1:4.

[18] Hebrews 12:14.

[19] Ephesians 4:1.

[20] Ephesians 5:3–4.

[21] Ephesians 5:11.

[22] Romans 12:1.

[23] Romans 12:2.

[24] 1 Peter 1:14–16.

[25] The word is translated *fashioning* in Peter's epistle and *conformed* in Paul's. More will be said about this word later.

[26] Ephesians 4:17.

27 Romans 12:2.
28 1 Peter 1:14–15.
29 *BDAG*, s.v. ἀναστροφή.
30 Hebrews 12:10. God chastens a man so that he will be a partaker of God's holiness.
31 Ephesians 4:23.
32 Romans 12:2.
33 1 Peter 1:13.

Chapter Two
34 1 Corinthians 9:9, quoting Deuteronomy 25:4.
35 1 Corinthians 9:9–10.
36 *International Standard Bible Encyclopedia*, Revised Edition, eds. James Orr, Melvin Grove Kyle, et al. (Grand Rapids: Wm. B. Eerdmans Publishing Co., 1939) S.v. "Agriculture," by James A. Patch. Part of BibleWorks, LLC © 2001, version 5. Hereafter, this work will be abbreviated *ISBE*.
37 The word *corn* in the Bible was a generic term and can be understood to roughly equal the modern English word *kernel*. When English settlers found a new grain cultivated by the Indians of the New World, they simply assigned it a generic term already in common use. See en.wikipedia.org/wiki/Maize.
38 Isaiah 55:8.
39 *ISBE*, s.v. "House," by Arch. C. Dickie.
40 *Hebrew-Aramaic and English Lexicon of the Old Testament*, by Francis Brown, S. R. Driver, and Charles Briggs. S.v. מַעֲקֶה. Part of Bible Works, LLC © 2001, version 5. Hereafter work will be abbreviated *BDB*.
41 parapet. Dictionary.com. The American Heritage® Dictionary of the English Language, Fourth Edition. Houghton Mifflin Company, 2004. dictionary.reference.com/browse/parapet (accessed: December 11, 2007).

Chapter Three
42 Exodus 20:14.
43 Proverbs 6:33.
44 Matthew 5:27–28.
45 While looking to lust is every bit a sin, merely the mental sin seems to have different consequences than does the physical act. In regards to the ministry, merely looking to lust after a woman does not, in itself, disqualify a man. It is potentially possible to look with lust, repent, receive forgiveness, and go on living without all the negative consequences of physical adultery. In order not to repeat the sin, however, there must be some changes made in the individual's life.
46 Exodus 28:22.
47 Isaiah 47:1–3.
48 See Leonard Verduin, *The Reformers and Their Stepchildren* (Grand Rapids, Mich.: William B. Eerdman's Publishing Co., 1964).

Chapter Five

49 Romans 3:23.
50 Genesis 39:2–6.
51 *Ibid.*
52 Genesis 39:7.
53 See the following Scriptures for similar usage: Genesis 19:32; 30:15; Exodus 22:16; Leviticus 15:24; 20:12; Deuteronomy 22:23, etc. Many times this language refers to the sexual act outside the bounds of marriage, whereas the phrase *knew his wife*, at least in the Book of Genesis, often refers to sexuality within marriage. Cf. Gen. 4:1, 25.
54 Genesis 39:8–9.
55 *Ibid.*
56 Genesis 39:10.
57 Pharaoh, for example, tried to use this tactic against Moses during the Exodus; Sanballat and Tobiah attempted the same against Nehemiah hundreds of years later.
58 1 Corinthians 6:18.
59 2 Timothy 2:22.

Chapter Six
60 Matthew 2:4–6. The scribes were quoting Micah 5:2.
61 *ISBE*, s.v. "Pharisees," by J.E.H. Thomson.
62 John 4:25.
63 *ISBE*, "Pharisees."
64 Galatians 3:16.
65 Acts 17:11.
66 2 Timothy 3:16–17.
67 Acts 23:6–8. The word *both* in verse 8 seems to refer to the two concepts of *resurrection* and *angels*. The word *spirit* seems to be an explanatory word and not a third theological concept, allowing Luke to use the term *both* to refer to all three words.
68 Matthew 3:7.
69 Matthew 5:20.
70 Matthew 23:13.
71 *ISBE*, "Pharisees."
72 Matthew 15:8–9.
73 Matthew 23:5.
74 *ISBE*, s.v. "Phylactery," by Edward Mack.
75 Numbers 15:38–40.
76 Matthew 9:10–13.
77 Matthew 23:25.
78 Matthew 23:13.
79 Matthew 23:14.
80 Matthew 23:15.

Chapter Seven
81 Genesis 39:9.
82 Matthew 23:5.
83 Matthew 9:10-13

84 Matthew 12:1–7.
85 Deuteronomy 6:5.
86 Leviticus 19:17.
87 Mark 12:28–31.
88 1 Samuel 12:24.
89 1 Samuel 13:14.
90 Psalm 19:14.
91 Psalm 24:3–4.
92 Psalm 51:6.
93 Psalm 51:10.
94 Psalm 51:16–17.
95 1 Kings 11:3.
96 Proverbs 21:27.
97 Isaiah 1:11–15.
98 Hosea 7:14.
99 Hosea 10:2.
100 Joel 2:12–13.
101 Jeremiah 4:14.
102 Jeremiah 4:18.
103 Matthew 23:23.

Chapter Eight
104 Romans 14:1.
105 Romans 14:2.
106 The majority of the discussion is found in 1 Corinthians 8, though the thought continues into chapter 10.
107 Romans 14:5.
108 The cliff in the issue of whether or not to observe the holy days was probably a command to worship God, such as the one Christ quoted to Satan, "Thou shalt worship the Lord thy God and Him only shalt thou serve." In the minds of some, the celebration of a certain holy day was an integral part of that worship, while others simply endeavored to live every day as to the Lord.
109 Romans 14:3.
110 *BDAG*, s.v. ἐξουθενέω.
111 Romans 14:4
112 2 Peter 3:16.
113 Romans 14:5-9.
114 Romans 14:10–12.
115 Revelation 20:11.
116 Revelation 19:12.
117 2 Corinthians 5:10.
118 James 4:4.
119 Hebrews 13:17.
120 Other examples of spheres of influence would be institutions such as schools, colleges, mission agencies, etc.
121 Romans 14:13–15.

[122] *BDAG*, s.v. πρόσκομμα.

[123] *Ibid.*, s.v. σκάνδαλον. The English word *scandal* is a transliteration of this Greek word.

[124] Romans 14:16.

[125] Romans 14:17.

Chapter Nine

[126] Psalm 101:3. There are other principles in this psalm that I believe are more easily kept by the presence of my particular fence.

[127] Ephesians 5:16.

[128] Romans 14:22–23. In this passage, the word *damned* does not refer to eternal separation from God, but personal condemnation in one's own conscience.

[129] Romans 14:19–21.

[130] Hebrews 13:7.

Chapter Ten

[131] Hebrews 5:11–14.

[132] 1 Corinthians 3:1 ff.

Chapter Eleven

[133] The increasing popularity of certain celebrities has made their fashions popular among men. Often these fashions are directly tied to fornication, either heterosexual or homosexual.

[134] Deuteronomy 22:5.

[135] See the chapter entitled "The Cliff" for an explanation and proof of this statement.

[136] Genesis 3:21.

[137] 1 Timothy 2:9–10.

[138] *Greek-English Lexicon of the New Testament*, by Joseph Henry Thayer, et al. Part of Bible Works, LLC © 2001, version 5, s.v. κόσμος. Hereafter, this work will be abbreviated *Thayer*.

[139] 1 Timothy 3:2.

[140] *Thayer*, s.v. αἰδώς. Emphasis in the original.

[141] *Ibid.* The Greek words have been replaced by their most common English translations in the Authorized Version.

[142] There are two proofs of the fact that some parts of a woman's body are more sexually attractive than others. First, there is the testimony of Solomon in the Book of Proverbs, but particularly in the Song of Solomon. Secondly, there is the testimony of the styles of a sensual world system that designs clothing to flaunt certain parts of woman's body. Styles may change, but the exposure of certain parts of the woman remains a constant.

[143] *BDAG*, s.v. σωφροσύνη.

[144] 1 Timothy 2:9.

[145] 1 Peter 3:3–4.

Chapter Twelve

[146] Matthew 5:28.

[147] en.wikipedia.org/wiki/Rock_and_roll accessed February 26, 2008.

148 en.wikipedia.org/wiki/David_Bowie accessed February 26, 2008.
149 *Rolling Stone*, Feb. 12, 1976. Quoted in www.av1611.org/question/cqtool.html accessed February 26, 2008. Original emphases have been omitted.
150 *The Evening Star*, 11 February, 1993, sec. A, p. 10, quoted in www.av1611.org/crock.html accessed October 16, 2007. Original emphases have been omitted.
151 Allan Bloom, *The Closing of the American Mind* (New York: Simon and Schuster, 1987), p. 73. Quoted in www.av1611.org/question/cqtool.html accessed February 26, 2008.
152 1 Peter 2:11.
153 Romans 8:8.
154 CCM stands for Contemporary Christian Music. The term *Contemporary* refers to the fact that the style is not in the style of the classical composers or hymn writers of the previous century, but in the style of modern rock and pop musicians.
155 John 4:24.
156 Mark 9:22.
157 Mark 1:34.
158 John 8:44.
159 Mark 1:34. Emphasis added.
160 Luke 4:41.
161 Mark 1:23–25.
162 Acts 16:16–18.
163 Proverbs 20:1; 23:29–35.
164 Isaiah 52:11. Emphasis added.

Chapter Thirteen
165 Leviticus 19:28.
166 1 Kings 18:28.
167 *ISBE*, s.v. "Cuttings in the Flesh," by George B. Eager.
168 Leviticus 19:27.
169 Romans 12:2.
170 Ephesians 4:17–20.
171 *BDAG*, s.v. ἀσέλγεια.
172 2 Peter 2:7.
173 1 Thessalonians 5:22.
174 en.wikipedia.org/wiki/Tattoo accessed March 7, 2008.
175 Acts 19:19.
176 en.wikipedia.org/wiki/Tattoo accessed March 7, 2008.
177 *Ibid.*
178 *Ibid.*
179 1 Corinthians 6:19.
180 John 14:16.
181 1 Corinthians 3:17.
182 Psalm 139:14.
183 en.wikipedia.org/wiki/Tattoo
184 Romans 12:2.
185 *BDAG*, s.v. συσχηματίζω.

[186] www.encyclopedia.com/doc/1G1-94598397.html accessed March 7, 2008.

[187] This inconsistency has motivated some believers to formulate a standard that rejects pierced ears, not only on men, but also on women.

[188] Genesis 24:22; Exodus 32:3.

[189] Leviticus 19:28.

[190] Exodus 21:2–6.

[191] en.wikipedia.org/wiki/Earring accessed March 15, 2008.

[192] en.wikipedia.org/wiki/Body_piercing accessed March 15, 2008.

[193] Romans 1:21, 25–28.

[194] 1 Timothy 1:9–11.

[195] Romans 1:26–27.

[196] *Ibid.*

Chapter Fourteen

[197] 1 Thessalonians 5:22.

[198] 1 Corinthians 6:18.

[199] Matthew 5:27–28.

[200] 2 Timothy 2:22.

[201] Chip Ingram, *Love, Sex, and Lasting Relationships* (Grand Rapids, Mich.: Baker Books, 2003), pp. 39-43.

[202] James 2:23.

[203] Genesis 13:6.

[204] Genesis 13:8–9.

[205] Genesis 13:10–13.

[206] Genesis 14:12.

[207] Genesis 19:1.

[208] Genesis 19:9.

[209] Genesis 13:13.

[210] Genesis 19:4–5.

[211] See note 49 above.

[212] Genesis 19:7–8.

[213] Proverbs 23:7.

[214] Galatians 3:9.

[215] James 2:23.

[216] 2 Peter 2:4–9.

[217] 2 Peter 2:7.

[218] *BDAG*, s.v. καταπονέω.

[219] 2 Peter 2:8.

[220] Ephesians 5:3–4.

[221] Ephesians 5:11–12.

[222] Exodus 32:6.

[223] John 19:23–24.

[224] Mark 6:31.

Made in the USA
Charleston, SC
08 January 2010